BUILD YOUR LEADER IDENTITY

A PRACTICAL GUIDE TO LEADING AUTHENTICALLY
FROM ANY POSITION

SUZI SKINNER

First published 2015 for Suzi Skinner by

LONGUEVILLE
MEDIA

Longueville Media Pty Ltd
PO Box 205
Haberfield NSW 2045 Australia
www.longmedia.com.au
info@longmedia.com.au
Tel. +61 2 9362 8441

For the National Library of Australia Cataloguing-in-Publication entry see nla.gov.au

978-0-9943862-3-6 (print)
978-0-9943862-4-3 (eBook)

Suzi Skinner captures the essence of authentic leadership and makes it accessible and actionable. If you are looking for a practical guide to harnessing your unique leadership potential this book is for you.

– **Anthony M Grant PhD Director, Coaching Psychology Unit, University of Sydney**

Suzi and her team at Roar People offer something very unique in the Leadership Development and Organisational change space. Their focus on leadership as a way of 'being' rather than something we 'do' or 'know' has helped transform leadership teams to greater personal and professional success, more so than any other program I've introduced. Grounded in evidence based research, Suzi's programs unlock the mindset shift required to live a truly authentic and empowered leadership identity that can exist in all of us.

Over the past 3 years, I've had the pleasure of partnering with Suzi and her team as we embarked on significant organisation and culture change. The results have spoken for themselves. We've seen dramatic turn arounds in many business and culture metrics, including productivity, engagement, safety etc. As a result of the learning that our leaders take away from her programs and how they applied that to their everyday leadership identity.

Leaders at all levels is something many organisations are striving to achieve. True accountability, inclusion and unleashing the potential in all employees is an aspiration many organisations have on their agenda. To my mind, partnering with Suzi has enabled the organisations I have worked with to understand that leadership is an action, not a position, to gain a deep sense of self and being clear about their behaviours and belief.

– **Allison Salmon, General Manager People and Culture, SunRice**

Suzi Skinner has written a book that is strikingly practical. Best of all it shares wisdom that has been hard won, with insights gained by being 'out there' in the world and supporting leaders in an array of complex and challenging environments. As you will see, through this book on leader identity, Suzi has announced herself as a significant thought leader.

– **Dr. Gordon Spence, Course Director, Master of Business Coaching, Sydney Business School**

This original handbook takes us on a deeply reflective journey, helping us to recognize how our unique leadership potential is expressed through deeply personal values, principles and beliefs. With wisdom and skill, employing real-life examples and well-researched exercises, Suzi Skinner will guide you from when you first began to discover your individual leadership potential, through the arc of your career. Written in a practical, straight-forward style, it is as though the author is acting as your personal coach.

Identifying leadership as a 'way of being, which has a positive impact on others' – and leader identity as 'the authentic expression of who you are or aspire to be as a leader' – this innovative book is highly recommended, whether for CEO's or aspiring new trailblazers. It is also extremely relevant for coaching consultants working with top executives and managers to develop their leadership abilities and vision.

Encompassing a wide range of issues – from leadership derailers, to navigating organisational culture and entrenched institutional mindsets, through to managing diversity and exploring self-limiting beliefs – *Building Your Leader Identity* really does live up to its title and deliver on its promise. It reveals how to develop strategies to strengthen your leadership powers, as well as ensuring that you can create your very own distinctive leadership stories to inspire others. I completed all the exercises as I read through the book, and found them extremely useful and compelling. This lively and refreshing book will prove useful for cutting-edge executives, corporate visionaries and business pioneers at all stages of their career.

– **Dr Sunny Stout-Rostron, University of Stellenbosch School of Business**

One of the key points in this easy to read book is that developing leader identity is an on-going process, in other words, we do not become a leader overnight or after a single training course. Rather we continue to develop our leader identity through various transitions and life experiences. Suzi provides exercises and strategies to help people develop their leader identity in a positive way. The book is grounded both in Suzi's award-winning research and her professional conversations with leaders across the globe. Any leader at any stage can gain something from this accessible guide to leader identity.

– **Associate Professor Grace McCarthy, Dean, Sydney Business School, University of Wollongong**

Suzi has been working with our organization for a number of years and when I spend time with her I always walk away feeling more positive about what is to come. At times after listening to her speak or attending the Leadership ID program I have wondered how to bottle her so I can get her infectiously positive and pragmatic messages on leadership at every level to touch more people in our organisation. Now it's possible as she's published the book! Suzi has helped us redefine leadership from a complex and seemingly unreachable set of capabilities to 'having a positive influence on others.' Everyone is capable of this, and once they realise it through reading this book or attending the program, they step into their leadership potential. For some this has been life changing; they describe to me how they didn't see themselves as a leader before the program, but the lifespan approach has helped them to identify themselves as leaders at home and in the community, and they can bring these qualities and strengths to work with them every day to lead from any position. I look forward to continue working with Suzi to unleash the power of more of our people.

– **Sian Mertens, Talent and Organisational Development Manager Kimberly-Clark ANZ**

Congratulations Suzi Skinner on creating a much-needed guide to leadership identity. This book will be my go-to guide in strengthening my own leadership potential and a highly recommended read for those I work with who want to gain greater self-knowledge and authenticity to create a ripple effect of positive change in the world.
   – **Dr Suzy Green, Clinical & Coaching Psychologist, Founder of The Positivity Institute**

Suzi is a delight to work with and her research based work not only challenges but also enlightens. I would recommend any individual or any organisation that is focused on developing individuals and as a consequence, building the capability of the organisation they work with to read this book or engage with Suzi and her team. Suzi brings oxygen into any conversations and her pragmatic energy is reflected in her writing.
   – **Darryl Prince, Regional Director People and Culture, Asia Pacific. ISS Facility Services**

As we progress in business it is good to take time to define how we present as an authentic leader and what good leadership looks like. Suzi Skinner has a formula that was ground breaking for me, helping me discover and reaffirm who I am as a leader in my role today. For anyone curious about leadership *Build Your Leader Identity* is a MUST READ!
   – **Clare Cahill, Creative Cloud Marketing Manager, Asia Pacific at Adobe Systems Pty Ltd**

Suzi has a natural talent for empowering people to bring out their best in their own style. This builds energy in people and their teams rather than burning them out. Not only is her work and writing in Leadership Identity research-based and sound, but she embodies it herself. Suzi is humble and kindhearted while poised, courageous, and compelling. Suzi is a natural relationship builder and a true pleasure to work with.
   – **Blair C. Relf, Ph.D., CEO, Motivational IQ**

Build Your Leader Identity integrates current research and practice in a user-friendly way to support anyone in organisations on the leadership journey. Suzi skinner provides an easy to read and even easier to use integration of theory, evidence base, and practical approaches to leadership development. A must read for anyone interested in supporting both performance and people within our current complex organisational contexts.

 – **Dr Sean O'Connor PhD, Lecturer Researcher Coaching Psychology Unit, University of Sydney**

Both insightful and helpful, with gifts of wisdom from years of research combined with many practical tools to work with and develop your most powerful and authentic leadership identity.

 – **Heather Dawson, Head of Business Development, Australasia at Morningstar**

Congratulations! You are a leader (even if you don't know it yet). Organizations are expecting leadership from all levels, even from those who don't carry a title. This book teaches you – and anyone – how to be a leader no matter where you work. You don't need a magic formula either, this book helps you identify your own leadership identity and bring it to life in your organization, and your life. Anyone can be a leader, with this book's help!

 – **Brian O. Underhill, Ph.D., Author,** *Executive Coaching for Results: The Definitive Guide for Developing Organizational Leaders*, **Founder and CEO, CoachSource**

The Author

 Suzi Skinner, M. App. Sci. (Coaching Psychology), is a researcher, facilitator, executive coach practitioner, and the managing director of Roar People, Selftalk Pty Limited – a boutique consultancy in Sydney, Australia. Suzi works internationally with organisations to transform leadership, accelerate change toward more inclusive workplaces, and enhance employee engagement. Suzi is a Harnisch Scholar and her research, entitled 'Understanding the Importance of Professional Identity and Gender in Developing Women Leaders', was awarded the first prize at the 2012 annual conference of McLean Hospital and Harvard University's Institute of Coaching. An aspect of this research has been published in the academic peer-reviewed journal, *Coaching – An International Journal of Theory, Research and Practice* in 2014. Suzi coaches and facilitates at executive and board level in a range of leading organisations, both locally and internationally, and is currently doing her PhD to extend the knowledge of how leaders are formed.

Contents

Introduction

Build Your Leader Identity puts people's sense of self at the heart of leadership and challenges mainstream theories that assume leadership is a state of mind or an identity that people have already established. By contrast, this book questions to what degree people see themselves as leaders in the first instance and asks how strongly their views on leadership are connected to their sense of self. It's a personal perspective that asks you to define leadership on your own terms in a way that is personally meaningful. This is a perspective I believe has been undervalued, until now.

This practical guide begins by asking you to embrace a new leadership mindset and to consider how your identity as a leader, as expressed through your core values, principles, and beliefs, is the foundation for the different types of leadership approaches you may take. This new mindset requires you to think differently about leadership and your own potential to lead. The approach reflects an important evolution from leadership models prevalent today which focus on aspirational behaviours and skills, by recognising the qualities of leadership you *already have*. It reflects an individual approach to leading which asks you to acknowledge these qualities and to define leadership your way, regardless of what position or level of management you may be in.

Taking a leader identity approach involves a process that will help you unlock your unique interpretation of leadership, freeing you to take the initiative, make better judgements, and connect with others in ways that are meaningful to you. It is a powerful perspective that will help protect you from 'derailers' or obstacles in your career; something that I think is increasingly relevant in an era of rising job uncertainty and employee disengagement. As such it represents an evolution towards shared leadership that can empower every individual to lead in the area they choose. It will also contribute to your career longevity, stability, and wellbeing in the workplace.

My leader identity approach is based on thousands of hours of conversations with senior business figures in my work as a leadership facilitator and executive coach. This has taken me across Australia, to the United States, Europe, and India. It is underpinned by my research, which won first prize for an academic poster at McLean Hospital and Harvard Medical School's Institute of Coaching in 2012, as well as by emerging studies from around the world that challenge traditional, command and control models of leadership.

By focusing on leader identity, I hope to encourage each of us to stop expecting so much from people at the top of organisations and to start expecting more of ourselves. Above all else, my ambition is that this book will give anyone who decides to go through the steps the opportunity to positively influence those around them, and to make a constructive contribution to their workplaces and the lives of others. My hope is that it will highlight how your individual interpretation of leadership – your leader identity – can empower you to make a positive difference in your area of choice, whatever your degree of seniority or career path.

Three core principles

In this book I want to start to change the way you think about leadership and the way you think of yourself as a leader. I make this statement because I fundamentally believe that whatever your background, your career, your life experiences, and whether or not you see yourself as a leader, the qualities of leadership exist within you right now. It is up to you (and to us together) to uncover them, recognise them, and celebrate them.

This is an important shift when we think about leadership because so many of us are still tied up in definitions that rely on having positional authority and people to direct. This approach is outdated and not really helpful to all of us who do not hold positional authority but who lead every day.

Importantly, in this book I make no reference to management and also no excuse for not covering this aspect of work. There are wonderful resources out there to help you manage; my intention is to help you *lead*.

There are three fundamental principles that we will cover and that will be repeated throughout this guide. I make no apology for repeating these key themes because as you will see, there is much work to be done in *undoing* the largely unconscious conditioning that has influenced your thoughts regarding leadership. This conditioning is a part of daily life, which we have all received and internalised to different degrees. The conditioning in the expectations in your culture, career, family, and social spheres can all impact on what leadership looks like for you or who you think should lead. My intention is therefore that by restating these three principles, they will become second nature to you by the time you have finished this guide. They will also help to underpin your success as a leader in whatever field or life area you choose.

1. The first principle is that the fundamental premise of leadership is to **influence others in a positive way**. Leadership is a social process and it is only through the influence on others that leadership comes to life. If we allow ourselves to get beneath the thousands of leadership models and approaches that fill our bookshelves and electronic devices, we start to recognise that the fundamental premise of leadership is influencing others in a way which has a positive impact.

2. The second principle is that **the qualities of leadership exist within us all**. Every individual has the capacity to constructively influence the people around them. This principle holds true, whether you are in a position of

hierarchical power or not. The positive influencing qualities of leadership exist within every individual, even if you may doubt your leadership potential or have not taken ownership of this aspect of yourself yet. It is up to each of us to recognise these qualities and choose to lead. By choosing to lead, I mean actively choosing to step into your potential and choosing to exert a positive influence on others.

3. The third principle is that **great leaders not only recognise their own qualities, but they also personalise leadership**. By personalising leadership, I mean that they give it meaning that is relevant to their approach and life experience. They have redefined leadership on their own terms and in doing so have taken a really authentic approach to leading. This personalising of leadership is what we term your 'leader identity' and it is different for every one of us.

Leadership as a way of being

Looking at leadership as a *way of being* is a perspective that complements the traditional personality and competency-based approach to leadership; however, it is not the same. Mainstream leadership approaches such as personality perspectives can provide very real insights into each person's tendency to behave in a certain way. Similarly, describing the behaviours of great leaders through behavioural competencies is also valid. However, these approaches do not tell the whole story. Instead, thinking about your life experiences, the events that have shaped you, and what you have learnt about leadership, helps capture the unique aspects of *you*. This perspective helps make sense of how you show up every day – of how you are *being* in your role and life right now. It is a perspective which sheds light on the experiences that have influenced you and that guide your daily routine, whether you are consciously aware of these or not.

Your leader identity is a fundamental component of your self-awareness. It is like the importance of self-awareness in your level of emotional intelligence (EI). As you may know, EI refers to your awareness in managing your inner emotional life and your relationships. It is a concept that has been popular for over 20 years. However, leader identity refers to your self-awareness regarding the various identities that you hold and whether being a leader is one of them. This level of awareness refers to your inner self-concept and how you see yourself. As humans, we are made up of many identities, all of which shape how we act. Your level of awareness regarding how strongly you identify as a leader helps us to understand whether you are fit to lead. Similarly, your life experiences influence what leadership means to you and in this guide we will explore together how you would describe this aspect of who you are and how your unique leadership comes to life.

In terms of understanding leadership and who you are being every day, a leader identity approach complements the personality and competency approaches. This is reflected very simply in Figure A:

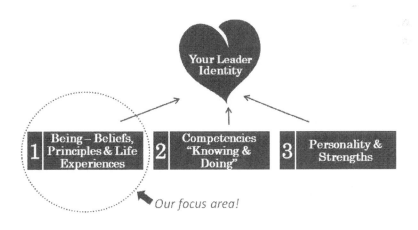

Figure A: A leader identity approach complements personality and competency approaches

With this guide I aim to give you some tools to capture your individuality as a leader and to be able to answer the following questions:

1. How could your career be enhanced if you were able to really take ownership of your own approach to leadership?

2. How powerful could it be to equip people around you with the insight and confidence to recognise and articulate their unique leader identities and to be able to work together in meaningful ways?

The applications for this type of insight and dialogue are endless, as you will see.

Leader identity model

The following chapters will take you through my evidence-based process for helping you to uncover and define your uniqueness as a leader and help you to build the career that you want. It is important to note that the approach outlined is grounded in the psychology and leadership literature. This is essential so that you can rely on the fact that whether you are working in business or at home, whether you are experienced in your career or just starting out, and all the other iterations of work, a leader identity process is relevant for all of us.

The research literature differentiates between the terms 'leader' and 'leadership'. The title of this book was originally going to be *Build your* leadership *identity*; however, this would have been an inaccurate representation of what this guide is about. To clarify, leader identity refers to the internal processes and characteristics which make up who you are. Leadership refers to the interpersonal aspects of leading which emerge in your relationship with others. So, for the purpose of clarifying our approach, we will focus on new ideas and perspectives that can assist your internal leader mindset and how this can set you up for success.

The leader identity process is outlined in Figure B. This model is based on the research I conducted over several years, which has been complemented with discussions and workshops with thousands of individuals around the world. This guide is designed to take you through this approach step by step.

Structure of the book

Chapters 1 and 2 will set the context for leader identity by taking you through the background of the approach and also explain why understanding your uniqueness as a leader is a prerequisite for career success.

Chapter 3 will focus on strategies to help you uncover your individual leader identity, and includes a series of exercises to help you do this.

Chapter 4 will focus on forming your leader identity and how this is a process of forming and reforming that continues throughout your entire career. Your leader identity is not one that happens when you first start working. In fact, it can represent a process of perpetual self-transformation.

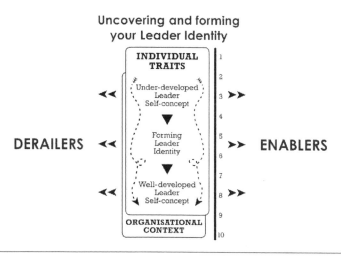

Figure B: Leader identity model

Chapter 5 covers research-proven self-enablers for building your leader identity, including strategies of personalising leadership and achieving authenticity, to strengthen this part of who you are.

Chapter 6 covers further self-enablers for strengthening your leader identity including your openness to change and adopting an inclusive mindset.

Chapter 7 will look at external strategies that can strengthen your ability to realise your leader potential. These include building your social resources and validating others – two key strategies which get to the core of collaboration.

Chapter 8 will look at the potential derailers in your leadership journey, and includes strategies to protect you from environmental and self-derailers in achieving your leader potential.

This detailed account of enablers and potential derailers is highlighted in Figure C.

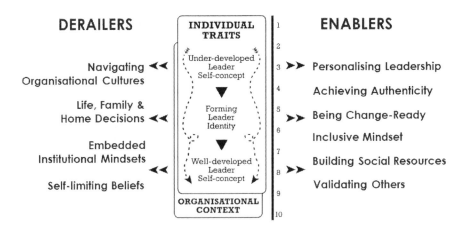

Figure C: Detailed leader identity model

Finally, Chapter 9 looks at how you can realise your unique potential by taking the exercises from this practical guide and applying them to your life – in whichever area is most meaningful to you.

The tools and perspectives to explore your internal expectations of what leaders may look like and to challenge yourself to step into your leadership potential are interspersed throughout this guide. In each chapter I have left space after each of the questions to allow you room to jot down your own notes. Together we will explore how you can tap into your uniqueness and lead in your own individual and compelling way.

Are you willing to go on this journey?

Chapter 1

Leadership is changing

The world is changing around us and our leadership practices are changing with it. Indeed, the way we think about leadership has evolved significantly in the first 15 years of this century. This has been driven in a large part by the requirement for more authentic leaders and better leadership across our economic, political, and social spheres. The need for leadership that transcends hierarchy and self-interest and focuses on the positive influence on others remains the challenge of today. In fact, if you read any of the best-selling leadership books, this need is central to them all. It is also the driving force behind a number of global initiatives whose aims are to assist organisations in creating a better world of work for their people and the planet. This broader context is the real impetus for this book and why your personal leadership approach is so essential. By helping you to lead in your own way, you will be contributing to building more authentic leaders everywhere – one precious person at a time. Who knows what a difference this could make to our world, our homes, and our communities?

Deloitte's *Global Human Capital Trends* report of 2015 highlights the urgency organisations are facing to develop better leaders. Their research involved surveys and interviews with business and human resource leaders from 106 countries. In it they highlighted that organisations are struggling to develop leaders at all levels and that whilst leadership is an urgent priority, only 42% of companies felt they had the necessary capabilities. Indeed, their report emphasised that leader development needs to be made available to people at all levels of the organisation. This was particularly relevant for the Millennials in the workforce, of which 53% aspire to lead. Encouraging and promoting leaders at every level is a paradigm shift for most organisations where the focus has predominantly been on senior leaders. However, an investment in leaders at every level would significantly close the leader capability gap, as well as strengthen the organisation's leadership pipeline.

The claim that the world is crying out for better leaders is also reflected in the epidemic of employee disengagement that organisations across the globe are facing. According to Gallup's *Employee Engagement State of the Global Workplace Survey* of 2012, more than a staggering 70% of employees are disengaged or actively disengaged from their jobs. This figure reflects the responses of participants from over 140 countries. In some countries the actual figure is even higher. Something is seriously amiss.

Working with individuals from all over the world, these epidemic levels of dissatisfaction in part stem from an outdated leadership paradigm that no longer suits the needs of workers today. The old paradigm of leadership refers to command and control principles where power and influence are exerted only by those at the top of the hierarchical pyramid. This structure means little power is shared by those at the lower levels. Within the command and control leadership model is an unwritten expectation that those at senior levels will anticipate and respond appropriately to the ever-changing needs of their environment, so that their organisations or institutions may survive. This model is seriously flawed when we consider today's context – where individuals will be exposed to the same amount of information by the age of eight as their grandparents did in their entire lifetime. The paradox of our working lives is that technology has made the physical tasks of work easier; however, it has brought with it a need to respond to complex decisions and masses of information in record time. We are now in an era where employees footnote their emails with a statement of when they will respond. This means that our expectations that those at the top will be across all of the information they have to respond to and will complete their decision making in appropriate time, is outdated and unachievable. Instead, everyone has a role to play in managing today's multifaceted environment.

There is also a growing research base into leadership which highlights how these traditional, top-down views on leading are being challenged and will ultimately be dismantled. Fundamentally, command and control is a leadership paradigm we have all been brought up with; however, it is important to recognise that it reflects a bygone era of industrialisation that focused on rules, regulations, and controlling employees. Whilst we have been conditioned to think of leadership in these hierarchical terms, it is actually a definition that is no longer meaningful for our collective futures. It is our educational institutions that are the driving part of this awareness. In a workshop involving team members of various ages, it was the Generation Y participants who confirmed that their university education had clearly set the expectation that hierarchical leadership was outdated. These participants were totally comfortable with the concept of leadership at every level; it was fundamental to their worldview. However, their straightforward reflection held deep implications for their generally older managers.

This gap in leadership expectations as being either hierarchical or shared, meant that the teams in this workshop went on to explore how different interpretations had an impact in their company. In this subsequent discussion, the younger team members were able to comprehend how their perspectives were not marrying with the current reality of their work environment. At the same time, more experienced team members were exposed to a different insight on leadership, which helped them connect to one another's expectations. If left unaddressed, this mismatch of perspectives could have resulted in ongoing tension within the teams. However, it opened up a rich, new dialogue regarding how leadership could instead be shared more extensively.

So, as workers become more skilled, more knowledgeable, and more connected, our leadership practices need to evolve with these shifts. In today's era of the knowledge worker, where employees are so much more informed and educated than in any other time in history, is it any wonder that they are looking for more? Perhaps you are one of them?

Instead of valuing hierarchies and principles of past decades, now is the time to evolve our leadership practices and to empower people at every level to take more ownership and to lead. Old paradigms need to be updated with new perspectives that are in keeping with our changing environments. Often this process can start with a simple conversation.

'Encourage-and-empower' approach to leadership

The trend of globally low employee engagement scores provides a powerful impetus for creating a new leadership paradigm which taps into the potential of people. The mindset of the future involves making leadership accessible to all people; whether it is within existing pyramids or decentralised structures. Finding ways for leadership to be shared amongst individuals is a challenge for any organisation.

We require an encourage-and-empower approach to leadership to satisfy the needs of today; this means that every individual has a role to play. From this perspective, leadership is not the sole property of those in positions of hierarchical power. Instead, it is something that can be exerted by anyone at any level. In fact, it is the people who choose to lead from any position (with or without positional power) who are making a difference every day. These people are everywhere, particularly if you are willing to look and listen.

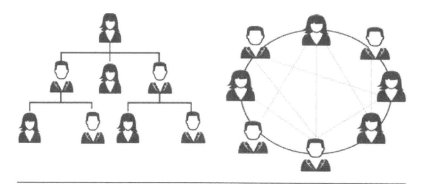

Figure 1.1: The evolution of leadership to an encourage-and-empower mindset

In a recent session, one of the team members talked about his belief in himself as a leader, regardless of the fact that he did not occupy a senior post or have anyone reporting to him. He personally embodied the belief that the ability to positively influence those around him was his, and he made a conscious effort every day to contribute. His contribution had not gone unnoticed. Instead, his peers were vocal in validating his approach and praised him for his constant positivity. This individual was also particularly insightful in being able to see where his contribution could have a positive impact on the business as well as the people. Thankfully, organisations are now starting to ask what involvement they should be seeking from all members of the organisation and how they should tap into the leadership potential of every individual at every level.

Creating a culture that recognises the leadership potential of every person is probably one of the toughest challenges facing companies today. However, research confirms it is worth the effort. Research by the Centre for Talent Innovation revealed that individuals are attracted to an inclusive culture that recognises the leadership potential of each team member and that these workplaces create more engaged employees with higher productivity. The research found that organisational environments which actively support their people to lead, to have input, to speak up, and to be heard, were 70% more likely to have captured a new market in 2013. They were also 45% more likely to have increased their market share.

The study identified six key behaviours that were exhibited by the team members in achieving these results. From an encourage-and-empower perspective (the new language of leading), they fell into two categories:

Behaviours of encouragement

- Making it safe for individuals to raise new or novel ideas

- Seeking feedback and actively implementing it

- Sharing credit for team success

Behaviours of empowerment

- Seeking diverse perspectives from all team members

- Ensuring everyone's view is heard

- Enabling team members to make decisions

The report calls these six behaviours the key to fostering a 'speak-up' culture. I call these behaviours fundamental building blocks of empowering every individual to contribute, to have a positive influence on others, and ultimately to step into their own potential to lead.

From an organisational perspective, Figure 1.2 captures this strategic link between validating and empowering a diverse mix of individuals to lead and improved organisational performance. The diagram outlines how empowering individuals to lead in a way that is meaningful to them but still gets the job done, is the foundation for helping everyone take responsibility for how they show up at work. This personal responsibility is a core characteristic of high-performing cultures where individuals and teams are empowered to take initiative and drive innovation and productivity.

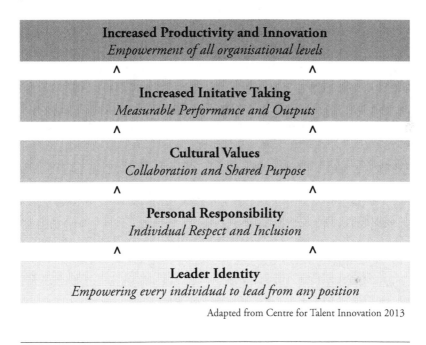

Increased Productivity and Innovation
Empowerment of all organisational levels

∧ ∧

Increased Initative Taking
Measurable Performance and Outputs

∧ ∧

Cultural Values
Collaboration and Shared Purpose

∧ ∧

Personal Responsibility
Individual Respect and Inclusion

∧ ∧

Leader Identity
Empowering every individual to lead from any position

Adapted from Centre for Talent Innovation 2013

Figure 1.2: Leader identity is a platform for increased productivity and innovation

Validating and empowering individuals from any level and from any background to have a positive influence on one another contributes to a strong culture of collaboration and cohesion. This diagram highlights that empowering more individuals to lead and building more inclusive environments require both strategic and individual change in order for it to be sustainable. This approach means empowering the individual but also considering the collective processes that may or may not allow individuals to step up. By validating the leadership potential of every individual and representing this perspective in organisational procedures, organisations can make a positive impact on the culture at large.

Those organisations that are consciously creating opportunities to share leadership are the ones that will enjoy greater engagement and productivity; it is already happening through simple changes. Organisations that are on this path are creating smaller, more empowered teams, budgets are being dispersed, and bureaucracy in decision making is being streamlined to provide greater autonomy and input to people at different levels. Here's a sample list of activities one global organisation decided to perform to empower more people to lead: reduce hierarchical communications, provide rolling leadership opportunities in all meetings, increase cross-functional secondments, and recognise individuals who show leadership at all levels.

The impact of change

The prevalence of employee disengagement is compounded by the continued and accelerated change in the lives of individuals everywhere. At a conference in Prague where I presented my research in 2013, I had the pleasure of listening to a presentation by experts from the Centre for Future Studies in Copenhagen. Their research predicted that by 2030, the world would be facing change on an *exponential* scale. Economic models, politics, generational patterns, work customs, and social connectivity are all expected to be transformed over the coming years. We can already see evidence of this as teams become more ethnically and age diverse and generations work longer. Importantly, this ongoing change is predicted to occur against a backdrop of economic uncertainty and turbulence that is already becoming the hallmark of daily life in this century. Indeed, 74% of organisations surveyed in the Deloitte's 2015 *Global Human Capital Trends* report believe their work environments are complex.

So, what does it mean for the wellbeing of workers if change and complexity is not only commonplace but also expected to accelerate? If you ask teams today about their appetite for change, you will hear everything from 'zero' to concerns about 'change fatigue'. A senior manager told me recently, "We had just completed another organisational restructure and one of my direct reports asked whether it was the last one. I responded that it was – until the next one. He wasn't happy." Not surprisingly, research by human resource and management professor Wayne Casio, from the University of Colorado, cites change as a key factor in employee disengagement.

Yet change is everywhere. Research by Egon Zehnder, a global recruiter, highlights that in today's world, individuals will experience an average of 11 careers or jobs in their lifetime. This is compounded by the fact that senior leaders are now expected to change their roles every three to four years. In a session with an IT team recently, team members spoke of the constant pressure and workload that they were under due to the ever-relentless change. They were facing the fifth organisational restructure in less than four years, and it hadn't been managed well. As a local team, they were hampered by the machinations of their global parent and the ambiguity of the restructure was causing both a lack of role clarity at a local level and an increased workload. Lack of trust was at the centre of their problems as they couldn't provide anyone with any level of job security.

So, is it any surprise that change has the potential to disengage? As humans, we are creatures of habit. We have a preference to stay within our comfort zones and to maintain the status quo. It is common knowledge within organisations that change initiatives are often met with resistance and cynicism. When change is not managed well, people tend to respond territorially and from a position of fear – worrying about their individual security and what they may lose, versus the potential for new learning or upskilling.

Being able to equip individuals to handle change and its resultant complexity is a fundamental requirement for organisational performance and employee wellbeing. However, it requires a shift in mindset. The table in Figure 1.3 comes from a presentation by the aforementioned Centre for Future Studies in Copenhagen. It highlights the conversion in attitudes that needs to be made; from the *old* mindset of work to the *new*. Rather than meeting these new challenges with an old hierarchical mindset, the column on the right articulates the new approach of the future worker that will be required to thrive in this changing environment.

OLD	NEW
Career	Calling
Employees	Co-Creators
Competition	Symbiosis
Time Stress	Intuitive Flow
Separation	Hyper Connection

Adapted from Centre for Future Studies (2013)
Copenhagen, W.I.N Conference, Prague.

Figure 1.3: Shifting mindsets for the future

The points below summarise what each aspect of the new mindset means:

- **A calling:** This involves helping individuals move into roles which are aligned to their personal strengths and tied to their intrinsic (internal) motivations. Rather than being career driven, it asks you to think about what you would be doing if you were purpose driven. Similarly, if you think about your current role, to what degree do you get to operate within your natural strengths? Research from Gallup tells us less than 30% of employees get to use their strengths regularly so there is plenty of work to be done.

- Co-creators: This term refers to the role that every individual within an organisation plays. It emphasises that employees are active agents for change, and that every individual is a co-creator in the life of the company, given the influence they can exert on the people and culture around them. It asks you to think about what contribution you may be making and how proactively you are co-creating your own team culture.

- Symbiosis: This perspective asks individuals to transcend competitive stances that they can take with one another and to look for solutions that are mutually beneficial to the team, the company, and the planet. It asks you to think about the influence you have in your role, but more specifically what influence across functional boundaries you can have.

- Intuitive flow: This characteristic involves creating work environments where an individual's abilities are challenged to an optimal level and where time stress is replaced by a rejuvenating sense of focus and energy. We read everywhere about the competing demands placed on our time; however, this approach asks us to consider the times when we are most focused and to build these into our daily lives.

- Hyper-connection: This term refers to embracing the technological and social advances that will continue to make our world a smaller, more connected place. This means adapting a broader perspective where our actions no longer happen in isolation but require wider consideration of their impact. It is a reference to oneness as we each move towards a global network.

I have included these new characteristics for working in the future because each of these worker attributes is underpinned by a critical mindset shift. The forthcoming direction of work is one where individuals are required to *take ownership* of their callings and become proactive in managing their roles and their opportunities. Even in the face of uncertainty like the IT team were facing, there is room to help individuals take back control and find the areas that they can influence. The concept of thinking of oneself as a knowledge entrepreneur is the mindset of the future: taking responsibility for one's own growth and learning. However, this self-leadership is unlikely to happen unless you are clear about who you are, about what you stand for, about how you want to manage the change, and the legacy or impression that you want to leave. Without this inner clarity you may be at the whim of shifting circumstances which can undermine your confidence and your sense of self.

So, if individuals are to survive and thrive within this evolving multicultural, multi-age environment, they need to know their own leader identity. They need to be able to maintain their sense of themselves in the face of potential instability. In this changing future, having a clear sense of self provides the foundation for good judgement, taking initiative, and helping you to feel empowered to exert your own influence. With clarity of your leader identity, there exists an inner stability which comes with understanding who you are, despite the different directions in which you may be pushed or pulled.

In essence, these future worker attributes compel individuals to recognise and strengthen their own identity – equipping them with a personal foundation firm enough to withstand constant change. We can go as far as to say that without this inner foundation, an individual's actions can be both damaging and ineffective – like a ship without a rudder. In this evolving context, understanding your unique leader identity is required now more than ever.

Leadership at every level

Everything should be made as simple as possible, but not simpler.
– Albert Einstein

Leadership being available to everyone at every level is represented in Figure 1.4, through the work of Bruce Avolio, Professor of Management at the Foster School of Business, University of Washington. Bruce's simple diagram gets to the heart of the message in organisational contexts. Implicit in this diagram is the fact that our ability to lead is not determined by positional authority or power, but rather by our own willingness to stand up and be counted. The challenge is out there for organisations to create an environment where leadership at every level can be realised.

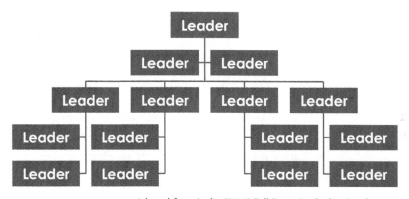

Adapted from Avolio (2010) Full Range Leadership Development

Figure 1.4: Adapted from Bruce Avolio: Leadership at every level

This perspective does not mean that everyone must aspire to a more senior position or a higher level in the hierarchy. Both of these aspirations reflect the hierarchical model of leading. Instead, the key to this approach lies in recognising that opportunities for positive influence exist *within* the structure. Leadership at every level means understanding that leadership is an action, not a position. It asks you to consider:

If you chose to bring more of your leader self to work, what positive influence could you be having right now, regardless of what position you are in?

A wonderful example of leadership at every level where leadership is defined as an action (not a position), was the winner of the Leaders Everywhere competition, which was conducted by *Harvard Business Review* and McKinsey in 2013. It involved a global call for creative ideas and case studies that actively encouraged people to lead from any position. The winning initiative was by the UK National Health Service, the world's fifth largest employer.

The background to the NHS initiative was the alarming statistic they were facing that 10% of people who came into contact with their services were harmed by them. A hierarchical response to this problem would have seen the creation of a series of top-down initiatives implemented to fix the problem via project streams and consultants and the like. Instead, the NHS took a different approach and decided to communicate the problem to their organisation without a predetermined solution.

In response to the communication, a small group of people without hierarchical authority came together with a common purpose of improving the service levels. The group comprised trainee doctors, administrators, and a range of assistants. Instead of seeking hierarchical support for this challenge, they corralled their peers and networks. Rather than proposing a pre-set range of solutions, they set up a website looking for ideas and asking for online pledges from employees to assist. As a first-year initiative, they were staggered to receive 189,000 invaluable ideas for improving patient care, each owned by the individual who suggested them. These individual initiatives were to be performed on a day that they would eventually call their Day of Action. It was their biggest day ever of collective action and evidence of the huge appetite for individuals to have a positive influence – in our language – to lead from any position.

A leader-leader mindset

Leader identity is a leader-to-leader approach which recognises that we all have the potential to lead. It also recognises that at the same time we are all followers. We may be followers of one another, followers of the purpose we have signed up for, followers of those who speak our truth, and so on. When clients say to me that the CEO is the leader, this old-model perspective opens up a wonderful opportunity for shifting this hierarchical mindset. Yes, the CEO may be the leader and they certainly do have the positional power; however, at the same time he or she is also a follower – a follower of the Board or the customers, their people, their industry, and so on. Many high-performing CEOs are keen to be a follower of their people and are eager to adopt their feedback for the good of the company. Recognising the leader-to-leader role that we can all step into is an important mindset shift. It reinforces and recognises that regardless of your position or title, you have the potential to lead as well as to follow.

Often this requires positional leaders in organisations to let go of the hierarchy and of control and develop new ways of tapping into the potential of their people. One IT organisation in Norway that was seriously struggling financially developed a series of activities where teams and clients were invited to 'speed date' the CEO. In these ten-minute sessions, the CEO had three questions:

1. What do you think I need to safeguard in this business?

2. What is so painful to you that you want to quit?

3. What talent do you have that we can capitalise on?

In accessing the views of every team member, the CEO was able to capture the uniqueness of their company and use this as a renewed platform to significantly improve their financial returns within a 12-month period.

However, shifting our mindsets on leadership is not an easy thing to do. In Prague, I saw this tension between the old model of leadership and the new one firsthand. It occurred in a conference session for Women's International Networking (W.I.N) that I was running, which involved women from 22 different counties. Prior to my session, I wondered how the concept of leader identity would sit with the attendees, particularly as English was a second language for many women in the room. As I outlined the new leadership mindset, it was a woman from the United States who questioned this view. She stated that leadership to her was about envisioning and setting a strategic direction. She emphasised her opinion by opening her arms up wide above her head, as though she were addressing a large gathering. And there it was! Her comments reflected all the characteristics of the old model of leadership, where it is defined as involving the big picture of organisations and of having widespread influence – something that is fundamentally only available to those at the top of the hierarchy. This hierarchical definition is not surprising, nor is its pervasiveness. It is the result of the hierarchical conditioning that we have all been subject to, particularly in Western cultures. Interestingly, it took less than 30 seconds for another woman from Poland to counter this view and state that for her, leadership was about helping others. She was a firm believer in the new mindset; that you didn't have to be in a positional power role to lead.

For me, this exchange was a great example of the current reality in which we are all working. Embedded within the hierarchical structures of our governments, institutions, and organisations are very real powers that exist for people at the top of the pyramid. However, the new paradigm asks us to recognise that leadership at the top and leadership that is shared is not mutually exclusive. In fact, they can exist in parallel. The hierarchy may be built to value people at the top but it does not necessarily detract from the power to lead that resides in the rest of us. If you are willing to shift your mindset and take ownership of your own leadership agenda, then you can lead by making a positive difference in the area that means the most to you.

Great leaders can exist at any level of your organisation or workplace or community or school. What makes these individuals 'leaders' is that they are able to act from the leadership qualities that they hold and they are active in helping those around them. This willingness to positively influence others through their own awareness and effort provides a platform of respect and inclusivity that can have a transformational impact on business. Unfortunately, this mindset is not a mainstream mindset today, so our job is to find these precious people and support them in driving further change. Perhaps, in reading this guide, you will join us in changing the dialogue on leadership and taking real action on this critical issue.

An example of how one individual connected with a core aspect of his leader identity was when he linked his role as a drummer as a teenager with his leadership today. He explained that, as a drummer, he provided the group with its backbone, ensuring that everyone was in time. His role was to effectively hold the performance together, even though he was positioned at the back of the group. He reflected that at a young age, he felt the weight of the responsibility he took on, particularly as the band played in front of audiences all over the country. Taking responsibility for the success of the group and providing a stable foundation for his team have been an unconscious part of his leadership. However, it was only through purposeful reflection that he connected these leadership traits to who he is today. This realisation helped him take full ownership of this part of his leader identity and to lead with greater clarity. He realised these traits have contributed to his success as one of the star sales performers in his organisation today.

Chapter 2

Defining leader identity

Leader identity is defined as the authentic self-expression of who you are or aspire to be as a leader. It is an aspect of your identity which includes the personal attributes, values, beliefs, and life experiences that you may choose to draw upon to define this aspect of who you are. Leader identity is an approach to leading that recognises the power of highly personal and individualised approaches to leading.

This individuality of leadership is reflected in the list of descriptions that invariably arise when you ask a group of people what leadership means to them. The list is always different, varied, and, from a leader identity perspective, correct – as long as it incorporates a positive influence on others. Here's a list from a session I recently held with staff of an entertainment company who were each asked to come up with one word that captured what leadership meant to them:

Guidance, influence, results, inspiring, fearless, respect, role model, patience, teamwork, continuous improvement, flexibility, charisma, vision, belief, support, motivation, courage, insight, inclusion.

There are always a few important reflections about this list. Firstly, no one ever talks about command or control; that language just doesn't come up. Secondly, the description that each individual lands on almost always differs from the next person. It is often different because it fundamentally reflects their own experience, or in our terms, their unique leader identity.

In this way a leadership identity perspective recognises that leadership is open to interpretation based on your own experience. It is defined in terms which reflect your life and the context in which you operate. Whether you see leadership as respect for others, driving innovation, or taking people on a journey, it is fundamentally a personalised interpretation which is as varied as the people who you ask.

Who are you as a leader?

I like this question because it raises a fresh perspective on leadership which recognises the relevance of leadership for everyday people like you and I. The fact that leadership is available to us all is reflected in a wonderful quote:

> *When leadership is defined not as a position that you hold but as a way of being, you discover that you can lead from anywhere.*
> – Zander and Zander, *The Art of Possibility* (2000)

If you define leadership as a way of being which has a positive impact on others, then chances are you do see yourself as a leader. However, if your internal model of leadership is tied to what we call the old paradigm, where leaders must have positional authority and a team of people reporting to them, then uncovering your unique leadership identity will need some work.

In *The Art of Possibility*, the authors, Rosamund and Benjamin Zander, make the very compelling case that everything we tell ourselves is a story – or *our* story, to be precise. This story is open to as many possibilities as we are able to conceive for ourselves. Being a leader is one of them.

Who are you as a leader? This question asks you to think more critically about how you define leadership or what leadership looks like to you. Invariably, your response is based on a range of factors; including your previous experiences of leadership, for and with whom you have worked, whether you see yourself as a leader, and whether you have influences like a position of power, work within a hierarchy, or have people reporting to you. Most people have never thought analytically about this question, nor have they been in discussions that revealed their differing interpretations or where these interpretations come from. The fact is that every one of us has a unique take on what leadership means – formed by our own life experiences and events.

Recognising the qualities you already have

The majority of leadership models today reflect the popularity of a *knowing* and a *doing* approach to leading by espousing the top competencies of great/effective/transformational leaders. The knowing aspect of these approaches focus on the knowledge that individuals need to gain in order to lead effectively. The doing aspect refers to a skills-based focus on leading – capturing the range of behaviours that great leaders exhibit. The intention of this work is hugely positive. There are very real knowledge and skills that people need to gain as their careers develop. However, the essence of people's uniqueness can often go untapped if the focus is only on aspirational skills and behaviours and not on the leadership qualities that are already in place.

Companies often introduce lists of leadership skills and behaviours that are representative of leadership in their organisation or what they aspire their leaders to be. However, these lists become problematic when you move from one organisation to another and invariably the list of requirements for leading in your new environment changes. Where does that leave you?

From a leader identity perspective, these lists miss the individual experience that each person represents. When I am shown the lists that organisations create, my first response is one of curiosity, as I ask questions which include:

1. Where is the recognition of the individual in these competency lists?

2. Where is the validation of the unique perspectives, beliefs, and backgrounds that each person brings?

These questions reflect that we need to enhance a competency approach to leadership by recognising the experiences and beliefs that have shaped each person and which inform their approach to leadership. We need to recognise that whilst leadership competencies are indicators of success in that particular organisation, a well-formed leader identity incorporates *all* of the precious experience that contributes to each person's authenticity as a leader, wherever they may work.

If you are struggling to reconcile my message of your unique leader identity with expectations from your workplace, consider the following two questions:

1. Have you been given a list of leadership competencies by your organisation on the type of leader they want you to be? This is often part of your performance review or you may have taken part in a leadership program which has been tailored to these competencies. This list of competencies is what we call the knowing and the doing of leadership for your particular work environment.

2. Have you been encouraged by your organisation (or by a manager or mentor) to define leadership in a way that speaks to you?

This is the *being* approach to leadership. This is all of your life experiences to date (including your life lessons/beliefs and principles) that have shaped your inner sense of yourself as a leader or who you aspire to be as a leader.

When I ask these two questions in seminars, I invariably receive lots of affirmation to the first question and an almost negligible response to the second. This has been the feedback from the programs we have run in Australia, India, and Europe to date. Most participants have never been in a leadership program that celebrates their uniqueness and that doesn't try to fit them into a box or competency list. Indeed, many participants have stated that not being pigeon-holed is one of the most liberating aspects of our leader identity approach.

The key to empowering individuals to lead and to creating more leaders is in understanding how the being perspective and the knowing and doing approaches are complementary. This lies in recognising the being aspect of each individual and embracing the skills and knowledge they need to develop. Here is how we reconcile these two perspectives:

This is who I am as a leader – based on my inner sense of leadership, my life experiences, principals, values, and beliefs to date.

AND

These are the competencies I choose to subscribe to in my workplace which will make me successful in this particular organisation.

Indeed, maintaining and refining your identity as a leader and staying open to adapt your behaviour to be successful in a specific context are the characteristics of great leaders.

So, should we be surprised that categorising leaders has been the default approach to training and development initiatives to date? There is great advantage in articulating what it takes to be successful in a particular organisation. However, what is equally valuable in today's context is taking individual life experience into account. What levels of engagement are we potentially missing out on when we rely on organisational competencies over and above individual experience?

To help bring this point to life, consider some snippets below of individual leader identity statements that participants in our programs have described:

"Driven. A starter, not a finisher. I juice the best out of every situation every day!"

"Acting in a respectful way, being inclusive, encouraging and striving to inspire."

"Being hands on. Expanding others' achievements and pushing them forward in achieving better things."

Notice the individual differences on leading that these statements reflect. These three statements reflect aspects of these people's lives and lessons about leadership they have learnt along the way. Where these statements become really powerful is in helping each person to link them to the stories, experiences, and beliefs that have shaped them. The fact that each person lands on a different aspect of leadership tells us more about their background. Each is *correct* in its own way; however, more importantly, each speaks to their authentic life experience – to who they are being as leaders.

Benefits of personalising leadership

I have had the privilege of listening to the unique leader identities of so many individuals through my work, and every time they are inspiring. One woman was in tears as she acknowledged for the first time in her 40-year career that she was a leader – she had never given herself the permission to take on this identity. She had come to this realisation after spending time in reflection and as a result of various development pursuits, including our Leadership I.D. workshops. Here is a little of what she had to say in one of the workshops:

> "As a leader you will see me finding solutions by connecting to the right people and establishing deep connections with others. My identity lies in creating networks of support and valuing relationships".

The sentiments she shared about connecting to others were gleaned from her unique experiences; however, it was her authentic sharing that caught people's attention. The room was silent in appreciation of her openness. As she spoke, you could hear the emotion in her voice as she outlined what leadership meant to her. Afterwards, another workshop participant stood up with tears in her eyes and declared:

> "If my manager had shared with me what leadership meant to him when I first started working for him, it would have completely transformed how I felt about my work, and my entire career. Things could have been so much better because I would have known where he was coming from!"

As you can see in this heartfelt response, this is important information. Being able to articulate what leadership means to you and what is important to you about leading is an aspect of self-awareness that is fundamental to your career success because it tells people who you are and what they can expect from you. It is the foundation for trust.

Yet this type of insight and dialogue goes missing every day. One global recruiter estimated that less than 10% of their candidates could describe who they were as leaders, even when they were in the position for a new role! The recruiter stated that these senior candidates – who were often already in leadership roles – didn't have the self-awareness to capture their leader identity. This gap is pretty meaningful when you consider that these candidates didn't have the language to describe how they were showing up every day. Imagine what a difference their awareness and sharing could have made to the people around them.

The importance of being able to share who you are and what people can expect from you, has so many different implications. One client mentioned that it was in interviewing a candidate for a role that her moment to share her leader identity arose. The candidate had one simple question: What could he expect from her if he decided to take on the role? In that moment the client was able to respond quickly and authentically, giving him a detailed insight into her own expectations for leading.

To help bring the different applications for leader identity to life, consider the following scenarios:

You have a new director who has recently joined the business and to whom you will be reporting. Your initial interactions with him are friendly and productive. Within a couple of weeks, you start to notice his drive for pushing the team (including you) to deliver more, faster, and with less support. Of course you are up for the challenge, yet it feels uncomfortable. Rumours begin that this manager is just in it for himself and you start to wonder if you have a narcissist on your hands. You can see the questions in your team members' eyes, but no one says a word. Gradually the team's performance starts to deteriorate.

What if this scenario had started differently? What if, at your first interaction, he said something like:

"I know you will need time getting to know me, so let me give you a quick heads up. I'm passionate about making a difference and leading this team to even greater performance. I'm probably one of the most competitive people that I know and I really care about winning. I also have a very strong work ethic. These are the values and principles of leadership I stand by. I know they are not necessarily shared by you all, so I am keen to understand what leadership means to you. My hope is that together we can draw on one another's experiences and really make a difference."

Or this scenario: You're about to have a high-stakes meeting involving a really important conversation with one of your colleagues. You feel strongly about the issue and recognise that it could have a potentially huge impact on the business, and ultimately, your career. You have done your due diligence on the issue, have asked questions, and gained insight into your colleague's position. You are so organised that you have sent through an agenda so that the two of you can stay on track. Once in the meeting, you find that the conversation turns difficult. You feel your temperature rising and your stomach tighten as the dialogue begins to falter. Luckily you are very present and you recognise that you have been in this situation before. You know you are not going to fall into a fight-or-flight situation. Instead, you take a different tack. Rather than going head to head on the issue, you decide to share with them more about yourself. Perhaps it sounds a little like this:

"I really want you to know how strongly I feel about this issue. This is about leadership and to me leadership is about collaboration. I believe if we don't open the communication to clients we will be missing vitally important feedback. I stand for openness and transparency. These are principles you can always expect from me. What are the principles you stand for? And how can we find a way forward together?"

When we encourage individuals to define their own approach to leading, we positively influence:

- Inclusiveness. By asking individuals to name what leadership means to them, we are opening up leadership to the vast diversity of individual life experience that every human represents.

- Engagement. When we allow individuals to put their own stamp on leadership, the likelihood for enhanced engagement – versus individuals feeling inauthentic – becomes higher. In doing so, we minimise the risk that they do not identify with prevailing leadership norms, particularly if it is defined in organisational, de-personalised terms.

- Motivation. Research shows that individuals are more willing to persevere in a leadership capacity if they feel like they have a choice in how leadership is enacted.

The current lack of appreciation for the role of leadership identity and personalising leadership is a potentially major blind spot in many leadership development initiatives. It may also be part of the reason that, according to McKinsey (2013), so many leadership interventions fail.

It is not easy articulating who you are as a leader, or who you aspire to be. Often it takes different experiences and sometimes a fair share of hard knocks to really help you uncover the principles, beliefs, and values that form the core of who you are. There are some fantastic exercises to help you to increase your self-awareness and to accelerate this journey; following the steps in this guide is part of this journey.

Small acts of leadership

In focusing on leader identity, I am taking a deeply personal approach. Discovering your unique interpretation of leadership is both empowering and necessary. You have an opportunity to empower the people around you and make a positive difference in your unique way, no matter how small these acts may seem. Consider for a moment:

- How often have you changed one person's perception of what they are capable of? This may be in the way that you listen to their needs or the feedback that you give that helps them see possibility when they did not.

- Or it may be in the everyday ways that you let others know how much they are cared for or valued.

- It may be the way you make an effort to say hello to everyone in the morning or the simple but heartfelt *thank you* that you provide on a regular basis.

These are the simple ways you can have a positive influence on others and lead.

A recent client experience typifies the promise of a well-formed leader identity. Having been promoted to CEO of a multinational organisation, this newly appointed leader faced the challenging task of filling the shoes of an autocratic and divisive predecessor. He was clear from the outset that his leadership would reflect his strongly held belief in collaboration rather than following the previous directive leadership style. As he explored and articulated his identity further, it became clear that it was grounded in principles of inclusion, hard work, and valuing input from every individual – principles he had learnt as a young boy playing baseball. His personal interpretation of leadership involved opening up the dialogue with each team member and finding ways to partner with them, locally and internationally. By redefining this aspect of his identity – within the context of his new role – he was then diligent in applying it to every interaction. Tardiness to meetings from his senior team was addressed by noting the impact the delay caused in making collaborative decisions, silo mentalities from various divisions were diffused in the spirit of partnership, invitations from international counterparts were sought for their contribution to better practice, and so on. In applying his personal interpretation of leadership in his daily work, he was able to fast-track the rebuilding of trust and cohesion within the organisation in record time. The power of his unique leader identity created a firm foundation for future success.

As you can imagine, there are so many different and positive leadership styles that it is almost impossible to capture them all here. However, regardless of style, successful leaders understand the importance of having a clear and consistent leader identity which can enhance their career success and longevity. These leaders have strong self-awareness, take responsibility for their actions, and ultimately are not afraid to be themselves. Importantly, like in the CEO example, they don't conform to the latest leadership thinking or models. Rather, successful leaders know who they are, what they do, and why they do it. That is, they know their leader identity.

The research base

The concentration of this guide on the importance of recognising and building one's leader identity was brought to my attention through my own research into understanding how senior managers navigate their roles in organisations. My research focused on senior women in large organisations working within three levels of the CEO. The differentiator of my research was the requirement that they had worked with an executive coach within the preceding two years. Using a grounded theory approach, I conducted in-depth interviews with senior women and analysed their professional and personal development experiences. My purpose was to explore whether any developmental commonalities were evident across their experiences and what we could learn from this.

The findings that emerged revealed that despite the individual differences of the interviewees in industry, personal background, age, ethnicity, and careers, each was to some degree defining, or refining, their leader identity. The focus of their coaching development had not been on their capability of doing the job. This skills or knowledge-based focus is often considered a traditional domain of coaching. Rather, their focus was on who they were *being* as leaders and how they were showing up. Here are a couple of direct quotes which hinted at this underlying dynamic:

"I think one of the biggest things has been developing my sense of self. I have a pretty good idea of who I am personally, but developing my professional self has been a really interesting exercise."

"When I took on this senior role, this is where I had the debate (with myself): Do I have to change my essential self to be successful?"

Whilst each participant had worked with a different coach, a different setting, and with a range of different challenges, they were each clarifying, refining, or building their personalised interpretation of leading. It was this aspect of owning their leader identity that gave them the confidence and clarity for their ongoing success. These findings are aligned with research by Herminia Ibarra, a professor at INSEAD, who found that having a clear and consistent professional identity was fundamental to career success and was linked to promotion and resilience.

An identity approach to leadership is currently emerging and is informed by a growing body of research around the world. Research by Lord and Brown (2005) found that for individuals to become leaders, their leader identity must become a central part of who they are. In other words, successful leaders have a really well-formed sense of this aspect of their identity. Their perspective reiterates that leadership is far more about *who* leaders are (*being* leaders), not just what they *do* (skills of a leader) or *know*.

Leader identity is also supported by Social Identity Theory. From this perspective, individuals adopt various social roles that they internalise and to which they give their own meaning. This helps make sense of all the different identities that you and I hold. Depending on the needs of their environment, individuals will call upon these various role identities as they are required. When parenting is the focus, an individual's identity as a *parent* may dominate. In a work environment such as a law firm, an individual's professional identity as a lawyer may be activated. Identifying oneself as a *leader* is another social role that individuals can adopt and one which is open to the personalised meanings that they ascribe to it.

Here's a snapshot of some of the key perspectives we have covered so far:

- Leadership is a social process that involves having a positive influence on others.

- Leadership is an action, not a position. It is a way of being.

- Everybody has the potential to be a leader – the difference is whether you are aware of this aspect of your identity and whether you choose to step into your leadership potential.

- Leader identity is linked to career success, longevity, and promotion.

Sometimes reflecting on how our earlier experiences have shaped our identities is not a comfortable thing to do. In one seminar, a man reflected on his mother's passing in his teenage years. He recounted that at his mother's funeral, he had become upset by a comment made by one of the guests. His father saw the interaction and promptly sent him to his room, with the instruction not to return until he had come up with two positives that he could retell. As you can imagine, he was horrified with this turn of events, particularly on such a dreadful day. And yet, he went to his room and returned some time later with two positives. His positives? 1) He never thought he would learn how tragic life could be at such a young age, and 2) if this didn't kill him, nothing would. What is remarkable about this story is that his resilience and optimism are legendary within his company. Yet he had never made the connection to how these characteristics were shaped. In addition to that, his colleagues were both astounded and grateful to understand this hugely meaningful part of his identity.

Chapter 3

Uncovering your unique leader identity

To help you uncover your uniqueness as a leader, it is useful to reflect on the career and life experiences that have shaped you up to this point. Purposively reflecting on the times in your career where you were satisfied or dissatisfied with the roles that you held can give insight into the experiences that have shaped you. This is particularly true when you think critically about why you felt the way you did and are able to identify the dynamics, principles, and values that may have been at play. For example, your satisfaction may have been:

- drawn from the impact of your first manager who may have led in a way which was in accord with your own values and beliefs; or

- derived from the culture of the organisation – perhaps the culture was particularly achievement oriented and this was a good match with your own identity.

In every case these are the experiences that have shaped your views both on what leadership looks like and whether you consider yourself to be a leader.

The fact is, we all shape and are shaped by our career experiences. They contribute both to our views of ourselves and our views of what leadership means to each of us.

Exercise 1: Career perspectives

To clarify what this looks like for you, we recommend you spend some time on the career perspectives exercise that follows. I would like you to grab a pen and jot down the following in Figure 3.2:

1. Horizontal axis: List in chronological order the positions that you have held over your career. If you have been working in the same organisation for a period of time, list the different roles that you have held. If you are currently on a career break, list this as another role or phase of your career. Some clients decide to go back as far as high school whereas others who have had longer careers decide to reflect on the past 10 to 15 years. It is up to you which timeframe you choose.

2. Vertical axis: Map your intuitive sense of how happy or satisfied you were in each of the roles you have listed. This is not an exact science but rather your gut feel at the time. If you were both happy and unhappy in a given role, try to find a middle point that reflects the overall experience.

3. Once you have mapped your roles and decided on your satisfaction levels in each of them, I would like you to write down the reasons why you have given these satisfaction ratings for each role. An example of what you may write is:

    Role: _____
    Satisfaction level: 7
    Reason: Good values fit with the organisation

However, I would like you to take this a step further and write *which* values were a fit. For example, was your satisfaction based on the fact that the organisation was innovative? People oriented? Philanthropic? The more specific you can be, the more meaningful this exercise becomes. In this exercise I want you to delve deeper and identify the key aspects of the values and the culture or the organisation that resonated with you, as these tend to be characteristics that mirror your own.

Clients often reflect on values fit, cultural fit, and organisational support as being key contributors to their satisfaction. One client realised her specific leadership foundations, stating:

> "The roles where I have been most satisfied were where I had opportunities to drive innovation and creativity. I have known this about myself; however, I hadn't made the link that my leadership identity is based on these concepts; particularly inspiring others to think differently. Wow."

It is also important to remember that even your least satisfying experiences can be your most formative. If you have some low points on your career map, I want you to think analytically about *why* this was a low for you and jot this down. A common reason cited in our workshops is a lack of autonomy. Others have cited office politics as a reason. I am sure you will be able to identify your own.

To assist you in completing this exercise, I have included Figure 3.1 as an example of my own reflections. As you can see, the diagram highlights times in my career that were great and those that were not so great. Personally, I learnt a great deal about the type of leader I never wanted to be in some of my low satisfaction periods. If you have been working for a while, like me, you can rest assured that you too have faced similar lows. However, if you are one of the lucky ones who are yet to experience a dip in your career (let alone a major derailer), then all power to you. I encourage you to take a quiet moment and acknowledge this to yourself. I also encourage you to keep reading so that you can learn more strategies that will protect you from future derailers that may or may not arise.

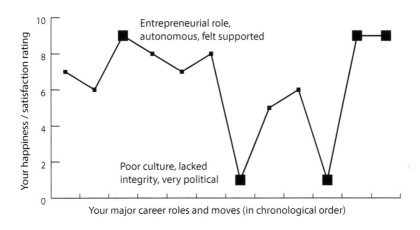

Figure 3.1: Career perspectives example

For now, please use Figure 3.2 below to map your own experiences:

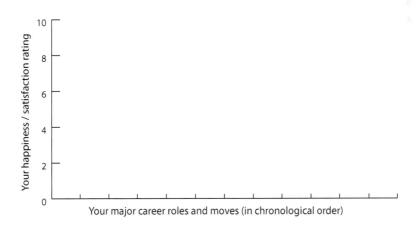

Figure 3.2: Career perspectives exercise

Exercise debrief

To get the most from this exercise, I encourage you to take some time to reflect on your answers and think analytically about what your satisfaction levels *reflect about your unique characteristics*. With this in mind, write down your answers to the questions below:

1. Which roles worked out well and why was this the case?

2. What patterns do you notice about yourself?

3. What do these insights tell you about your unique characteristics?

4. How did these roles and experiences shape your views on leadership?

Once you have done this, I recommend finding a trusted advisor with whom you can discuss the aspects of your career that have helped shape who you are today.

To take this reflection further, write down some descriptions of your unique leadership characteristics and principles in the space below. At this stage I expect your thoughts may be one-word descriptions or bullet points, which is fine. This is the first step in articulating your leader identity and one that we will continue to build on throughout this guide. Remember that any description you write down as a result of prompting from this exercise is valid – as long as it has at its core a positive influence on others.

My leader identity includes characteristics/principles/values such as:

If you have managed to get a few bullet points down, this is a great first step.

Exercise 2: Influences on your leader identity

A powerful takeaway of this influences on your leader identity exercise is that you start to gain insight into the uniqueness of your own approach to leading. In Western cultures it is important to recognise that there is a strong bias to what leadership looks like – particularly when it comes to gender. We will cover this male bias of leadership more comprehensively in Chapter 6; however, it is important to note that gender is just one of the biases we may have internalised over our lifetimes.

Culture example

In Australia's corporate culture, the sporting bias with leadership is particularly strong and representative of a core cultural bias when it comes to leadership. The bias is so prevalent that if you visit the boardrooms of certain organisations you will not be surprised to see signed rugby jerseys adorning the walls. These are very real symbols of those organisations' values when it comes to leadership. So, within this context, whatever sporting metaphors you can think of will probably sit well.

Similarly, in the United States, a review of the CEOs of Fortune 500 companies showed that less than 5% were shorter than six feet tall. What does this tell you about the implicit bias or expectations that Americans may be internalising when it comes to their leaders?

The questions below are designed to get you to think more broadly about leadership approaches that you come across every day. Interestingly, there will be people, colleagues, and friends whose approach to leading sits well with you. This comfort may signal a bias that may need exploring or it may be that this alignment sheds light on your own leader characteristics.

Take a moment to write down your responses to the following questions:

1. Who do you admire as a leader? (This may be figures in the media, family members, and so on.)

2. Which emotional, psychological, and behavioural aspects of their leadership do you most admire?

3. Are there any aspects of their leadership that you emulate or aspire to emulate?

4. Which individuals are not leaders in your eyes? Why not?

5. Given your responses to questions 1 – 4, how would you describe what leadership means to you?

If you get the chance, I recommend doing this exercise with your team or your peers. When we do this exercise in pairs or groups, the diversity of leadership interpretations that arise provides a wondrous smorgasbord to explore. When we take an identity perspective, we get to move beyond the conditioning of organisations or culture, and recognise that, in reality, leaders are far from a homogenous group. There is an unfathomable variety in age, marital status, family background, ethnicity, culture, and life experience. All these have an impact on each individual's unique interpretation and approach to leading.

When done in groups, this exercise is a powerful reminder that we must be open-minded and inclusive in remembering that everyone has their own understanding when it comes to leadership. If you choose to explore this with a group of your own, this exercise will give you first-hand experience of respecting the individuality of leadership. This broader perspective is critical to tapping into the leadership potential of the people around you and, in doing so, creating new and richer ways to lead.

Exercise 3: Lifespan approach to leading

Now, let's take this career perspective further by widening your reflection to encompass your life to date, to where you are right now reading this page. Take a moment to consider your leader identity in primary school, in high school, in your first job, into your 20s, 30s, and so on. The influence of contextual and environmental factors such as parenting styles and the sports you may have played are all relevant in forming your uniqueness. We are socialised by our interaction with our family, our friends, and others whom we trust and respect from our earliest age, and these have a powerful influence on our unique take on leadership. It is in these interactions with significant others that we learn stories, myths, stereotypes, and a vast array of information (and misinformation). This misinformation may be correct in the eyes of the person we are learning it from but eventually the information may turn out to be only part of the picture – or more specifically, their interpretation of leading.

We consciously and subconsciously accept stories and beliefs over our lifetime. Exposure to new people, different ideas, and cultural aspects such as media representations continues this process. Importantly, these exposures shape how we view ourselves and how we view others. Never has this been more accurate than our conditioning and expectations regarding leadership. For example, think of the way leadership has been presented to you in the media – who is in power? And what happens when those who don't fit the 'accepted model' take over?

This exercise builds on research by Murphy and Johnson (2011), which highlighted the various developmental influences that shapes each person's view of themselves as a leader. Figure 3.3 is adapted from their approach and highlights key early influences such as parenting style and education that impact on understanding your unique leader identity:

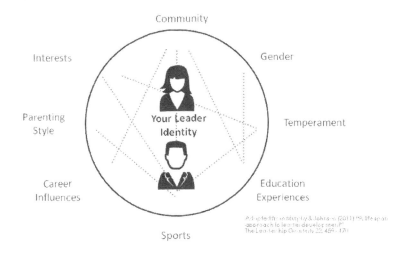

Figure 3.3: Early influences on your leader identity

Based on their research, these influences shape your views on leadership by helping you to form internal mental models of leadership. For example, if you were part of a basketball team where the captaincy was shared amongst your peers, then this may have formed an internal expectation that leadership should be shared today. It is these hidden internal models that determine whether you may or may not see yourself as a leader.

Building on your reflections of the career experiences that have shaped who you are, I now want you to take this lifespan perspective and consider all of the experiences where you have had a positive influence on others – both inside and outside of work. This exercise is designed to take you out of your comfort zone by asking you the times in your life, such as your teenage years and childhood, when you had a positive influence on others. As it is very rare for individuals to have had a positional role in this life stage (hallmarks of the old hierarchical leadership mindset), many people initially struggle with this task. However, what I am asking you to do is to drop any notion of position and to focus on the times in your earlier life you had *a constructive influence* on others – the new language of leading.

To assist you with what this can look like, here are some examples from our program participants:

Description of my positive influence on others	Leader identity characteristic this revealed
Working from age 13 in a business I created myself	Entrepreneurial; Autonomy
Looking after my younger siblings	Taking responsibility; Caring for others
Being a best mate	Loyalty; Valuing deep connections

It must be said that these workshop participants began the lifespan exercise with a healthy dose of scepticism. They were particularly concerned with how meaningful it was to their leadership to look backwards – particularly given that, from a knowing and doing perspective, we are always looking ahead. However, all of them were surprised at the power their responses held for them. In doing these simple reflections, each participant recognised how some of their most deeply held principles were shaped by these early experiences. One man spoke about breaking his leg in his teens and reflected that he was able to link how that difficult episode gave him a broader perspective that he uses regularly in his work today. He explained that he regularly reminds his team that whatever difficulty they are facing, there is always someone facing something far worse. This simple perspective-taking approach helps him and his team to stay focused under pressure. This characteristic of his leader identity is something that he relies on intuitively and yet it was only through this reflection that he could connect the dots in a meaningful way.

Another participant had totally forgotten her first foray into work, which was as a result of taking her own initiative. She was physically bolstered by making this linkage to who she is as a leader today. Her face lit up and she straightened her posture as she told the group her story of creating her own first job at the tender age of 13. Remembering her younger self and connecting to her entrepreneurial flair helped her to make sense of her recent career moves. She recognised she had been the happiest in roles where she was given the autonomy to make decisions and set direction. Importantly, in making sense of her past choices, she felt better equipped to navigate her future from a more confident perspective.

I am often surprised by the emotional reaction that individuals have to this exercise. It is in fact a simple perspective-taking practice that asks each person to reflect on who they were as a teenager. However, as we have seen, there is so much power in reconnecting each person to their younger selves and to giving themselves permission to acknowledge the best parts of who they were back then. From a leader identity perspective, there are wonderful stories and examples of each person's uniqueness that are often overlooked.

In another seminar I actually got goose bumps as a young woman just out of her teenage years did this exercise and realised that her leader identity was tied to her musicality. She was her best self as a leader when she was engaged in activities around dance and teaching. Of course she knew about her musical abilities; however, she had never made the connection to her unique identity around creating harmony and flow, and how this insight could help her shape her future direction.

Exercise 4: Leading in adolescence

The first stage of this exercise is to focus on the experiences of your teenage years where you had a positive influence on others. This is often a very formative stage and one where aspects of your unique leader identity may have been brought to life – either through positive experiences or negative experiences.

In Figure 3.4, the vertical column lists the different areas in your life where you may have had the opportunity to positively influence others, or, in our words, opportunities to lead. Once again, I ask you to remember the small things that you did that had a positive impact. Something as simple as baking your family's favourite cake is meaningful. This simple choice that you made may point to very important leadership characteristics such as enjoyment, fun, generosity, and creativity. Just like one of our participants who reflected that as a teenager she had a choice to lead every day by sharing her lunch with others. So simple and yet so powerful.

In this exercise, please note that I do not expect you to write an experience in every section. Rather, the value is in spending time reflecting on your past and on the times that really resonate with you. There are no right or wrong answers here; this is about the acts of influence that were meaningful to you. As you can see in the examples above, this exercise is more profound when you can link the experiences to specific principals/values/beliefs that speak to who you are (or who you aspire to be) as a leader today.

Areas	Adolescence
Family	
Friendships	
Parenting	
Sports	
Education	
Community	
Employment	
Entrepreneurship	
Associations/Clubs	
Politics	
Volunteering	
Arts/Music/Theatre	
Other	

Figure 3.4: Leading in adolescence

Now that you have identified times where you had a positive influence, the key is in identifying which leader characteristics these revealed in you. Note these characteristics below:

Exercise 5: Leading in childhood

Your childhood is also an incredibly formative time of your life. I have positioned this exercise after the teenage years exercise as it often requires even deeper reflection. Once again, I would like you to go back further and think about the times in your childhood where you had a positive influence on others. This exercise is not asking you about times when you changed the world but rather the everyday life experiences of your youth.

To assist with your reflections, I have included a couple of examples from our clients.

Description of my positive influence on others	Leader identity characteristic this revealed
Being the connector and 'go-to' person among my siblings	Listening; Empathy; Communication
Standing up for my friends at school in the face of injustice	Fairness; Courage; Independent thinking

These two examples stand out because they represent part of the everyday life of childhood that so many of us have experienced. The man who recognised where his leadership passion for standing up for others and being unafraid actually came from found this exercise empowering. He was finally able to consciously link his leadership attributes to a time in his life when they were formed or validated. Once again, this was an impactful insight for him; helping him make sense of the leader he was today and giving him clarity to keep making a difference.

Another addition to help you with this exercise has been offered by one of my wonderful colleagues, Heather. Heather suggests that prior to doing this reflection you should do a visualisation exercise which helps you think about these positive parts of yourself. Take some time to recall a time you felt you were at your best and had a positive influence on others. Place this book down by your side and take a few minutes in silence with your eyes closed to recall the experience. Try to remember the feelings of that experience and hold that feeling of strength and confidence as you open your eyes again. Write down your childhood experiences.

Areas	Childhood
Family	
Friendships	
Parenting	
Sports	
Education	
Community	
Employment	
Entrepreneurship	
Associations/Clubs	
Politics	
Volunteering	
Arts/Music/Theatre	
Other	

Figure 3.5: Leading in childhood

Taking this exercise further

Depending on your life experience, these exercises can be just as powerful when reflecting on every decade of your life through to the one you are in right now. What were the positive influences that you instigated in your 20s, 30s, 40s, 50s, 60s, and 70s? Most importantly, how do you take these influences and own them? How do you integrate them into who you are as a leader today?

A woman in one of our seminars in India stood out to me as she recalled that her leader identity was strongly influenced as an adult in her late 20s when she had her first child. She recounted that it was through this life event that she was reminded of her capacity of caring for another person, of putting someone else's needs before her own, and of being the custodian of another person's future. These were the qualities of leadership that she developed as a leader in her home and brought into her workplace. Her linkage of motherhood and leadership was made all the more poignant in the context of India's turbulent gender culture. This was a woman who took ownership of becoming a mother and celebrated its effect in shaping her unique qualities of leadership today.

How does this insight help you?

These exercises are designed to assist you in putting some language around what your unique leader identity may comprise. Most importantly, it connects you to the stories of where it was on display. Your challenge now is to select one or two stories which encapsulate this part of who you are and share them with your significant others. To start with, you may be most comfortable sharing these insights with your family. However, my intention is that you will be able to articulate some of these stories with your peers and your team in a way that helps them to understand who you are as a leader and to connect with this part of you. I encourage you to share what you have learnt about yourself so far. Taking ownership of your uniqueness is part of building your leader identity.

As you may have realised in these straightforward activities, you can learn to see your stories and to understand them more deeply. This is so significant because your past shapes who you are today. There is great wisdom that comes from learning from your past and using this information to build the future that you want. And perhaps, just as importantly, you are the creator of these stories. This means that they are relevant to you today and they are also open to being updated in a way that aligns with who you aspire to be as a leader. There is comfort in knowing that if you are the creator of these stories, you are also capable of modifying them in a way that speaks to your aspirations.

Leader identity in action

One example of the power of leader identity in action is in how individuals react in the face of job loss. If you have ever been in this situation, either by choice, by redundancy, or for some other reason, this is often when your identity is put to the test. Individuals can report becoming unstuck psychologically and emotionally, as well as financially. Indeed, when individuals realise that so much of their identity has been unconsciously tied to their company title and their role, losing their job can feel like a body blow or trauma. It is not unusual for someone to take months to regain their equilibrium and feel like they are themselves again. However, from a leader identity perspective, what does this reaction tell us about their identity?

When your leader identity is well formed, hardships such as losing a job don't cause a blow to your self-esteem. This is because there is recognition within you that whilst having the job was good, helpful, interesting, financially rewarding, etc., being without the job means opportunity. Opportunity to recalibrate, reflect, and tune into a range of other avenues that may become available to you. This perspective is fortified by the strong foundation of a well-formed identity – something that transcends where you work or the title you hold. Losing a job can be tough but it doesn't have to damage your sense of self.

To explore this scenario further, ask yourself:

If you lost your job tomorrow, would you show up in the same way?

The ability to handle challenges such as the all too common experience of redundancy is a showcase of leadership. The ability to handle these challenges in a consistent way is a showcase of your leader identity as is evident in the following case study.

Leader case study

Peter: A senior executive of a non-profit organisation involved in medical research.

Over the course of our working relationship, Peter has faced a variety of challenges – either supporting his team through various transitionary phases such as restructures and new CEOs to eventually facing his own redundancy. What was so reassuring about my relationship with Peter was that whether he was in a job or out of one, I knew exactly with whom I was meeting. When he was looking for his next role, we met in a cafe; when he was running the organisation, we met in the office. However, regardless of the change in setting, I still met the same person. Irrespective of what was going on in his team or his career, Peter's unique leader identity – optimistic, connected, and strategic – always shone through.

I am sure you can think of a myriad of examples where the benefits of having a well-formed leader identity are clear. Indeed, if you really believe that the qualities of leadership exist within every individual, then this can transform how you view yourself and others. It has done so for me. I am yet to be confronted with an individual who doesn't recognise the various aspects of leadership they hold. Whether they happen to be employed or not, in a large organisation or a sole trader, studying or on sabbatical, and all the possibilities in between, there is a certain knowing that comes when people are asked to disclose this part of who they are. As one woman said to me, "I am a leader of my family every day."

When you open up the dialogue and allow people to explore what aspects of leadership are already within their identity, you become a privileged witness to the amazing human spirit that resides within us all.

Articulating your unique self

These exercises may feel cumbersome to those individuals who don't have the time to reflect; however, engaging in self-reflection is vital to your wellbeing and success. In order to realise your leader identity and bring more of yourself to your chosen area of work, you must be able to define what you stand for and what others can expect from you.

As we have seen, prescriptions about what works for most leaders or what leaders *should* do have little relevance in our dialogue today. Our futures need to include our own personalised meanings of leading. Every individual has a unique set of circumstances and talents that can only be realised by taking a personalised approach. Taking time to answer "What does your leader identity look like for you?" is a key step.

One of the pleasurable aspects of my work has been to get to know some very special people who are going about their everyday challenges and win with their own unique identity. Here are a few additional steps that may help you in this defining your own:

Acknowledge the best parts of yourself

Everyone has the capacity to showcase the best parts of who they are. Acknowledging your unique values, strengths, beliefs, and expertise, and choosing to put these into action is a powerfully simple way for you to reinforce your sense of self. Asking "Am I showcasing the best aspects of myself at work?" or "What is one way I can apply my personal values this week?" are useful check-in points that can reignite a sense of your uniqueness and of realising your potential.

Scrutinise your day

Identifying the day-to-day situations in which you feel like you are not being true to your leader identity is another helpful exercise. On examination, individuals often realise that there are many scenarios where they have been true to their self. This realisation can challenge a common tendency to over-generalise or focus too much on the times when one may feel disempowered. Answering questions such as "In which situations does my leader identity show up?" and "When am I less than my real self?" can highlight a more realistic perspective on who you are. This reflection may also give you insight into a tangible path of action that is situation specific.

Articulate your thoughts

Any type of journaling is an act of externalising the inner gymnastics of your mind and getting perspective on your own thinking and stories. Research shows that reflecting on successes can reinforce a sense of positivity and assist you in coming to terms with aspects of your identity.

By getting into the habit of journaling and recording your thoughts in writing, you can more easily challenge your thinking and identify recurring patterns more accurately. There may be blind spots that you encounter every day that only come to life when you write down what you were doing and the degree to which your leader identity shone through. In this context, writing down your reflections is a positive way of taking yourself through your day and enhancing your self-awareness.

Be intentional

Defining and realising your unique leader identity requires conscious effort and action. Actions such as being deliberate about how you show up can be both challenging and rewarding. The more you choose to showcase your unique identity, the more powerfully these behaviours will be embedded into your day and validated by the people around you. As you will read, these actions will make it easier for others to connect with you and trust in you. Questions for you to consider:

1. How is leadership defined in your organisation? Which leadership behaviours are valued and not valued?

2. What does this tell you about the context you are operating in? Are there certain adaptations you need consider?

3. Which leadership traits/behaviours/approaches do you aspire to do more of?

4. How can you ensure your leadership approach is true to you as well as mindful of the context in which you operate?

Here's what one young woman said when describing her leader identity:

"My mother has been ill most of my life. All I have ever wanted to do is make her happy. And that's my leadership purpose; to make everyone happy."

Chapter 4

Forming your leader identity

How can we expect individuals to lead if they don't see themselves as leaders?

Over the years I have heard many clients lament that their team is not *stepping up* and taking on more responsibility. Often they have done all the right things, sending them to training or providing them with in-house programs to motivate them to lead. In many cases their frustration can be palpable as they come up against what they perceive to be inaction.

The willingness of managers to develop their team members is a wonderful quality and in terms of readiness for the complex future we all face, a worthy pursuit. However, the consideration of the individual's readiness for development is frequently unexplored.

Perhaps you have attended leadership training and found it didn't resonate with you? Or perhaps you have seen your peers attend training programs only to notice that it made little different to their mindset? This chapter is designed to give you insight into an underlying dynamic that may be at play.

Do you see yourself as a leader?

When I ask this question to audiences I tend to get a range of responses. At one end of the range of responses are those who definitely do. Further along are those who sometimes do and at the other end are those who just don't. This range appears in every group and every audience that I have asked over the years.

This variety highlights that people differ greatly in *the degree* to which they identify as leaders. Some strongly identify as leaders whereas others see leadership as something outside of themselves and quite foreign. Imagine sending this individual to leadership training with this level of (non-) leader identity. As you have seen in the earlier examples, every individual navigates life's path towards leadership differently. Given this, it is vitally important to respect the individual self-rating given to this question. This is because each response provides vital clues about their identity. An individual's response is dependent on many factors, including their life experience and what their unique views of leadership may be. And as you will see, there may be other activities that this individual could engage in prior to taking this training step.

This range of responses refers to the *forming process* of leadership that every one of us goes through. In the same way that leadership itself can be defined in individual terms, the process of forming your leader identity is also a very unique one.

To help explain the process of identity formation, the tree with the root system in Figure 4.1 is a useful metaphor. As you know, underneath the surface of any tree resides its root system. These roots are invisible to the naked eye; however, the degree to which they are entrenched in the soil indicates the strength and longevity of the tree. A well-formed root system means that the tree can get the nutrients it needs, can withstand the effects of the weather, and so on.

Figure 4.1: Tree and its root system, like your multiple social identities

Much like this root system, the identities that make up *you* are hidden; unless you are prepared to go digging. In terms of our metaphor, each root of the tree is like the various identities that are a part of you: your professional identity; your family identity, your friend identity, your sporting identity, and so on. We are all the sum of many parts and they are all intertwined. Each gives colour and character to how you show up as an individual in different contexts. An example may be identities such as partner/friend/manager, and so on. A leader identity approach asks you to consider whether *leader* is an identity you give yourself amongst this collection.

In my research, the interviewees did not focus on the skills they acquired or the knowledge they learnt in their coaching programs. Instead, they focused on forming their leader identity. The statement from one interviewee reflects the importance of this focus:

"I'm wondering whether part of our issue is stuff that's really quite deep and we can go to courses on how to speak calmly, lower your tone of voice, until the cows come home. But if you're not dealing with that inner stuff, you're definitely walking uphill."

We all hold ourselves to some individual expectation of what leaders should look like and to how we rate ourselves against our own expectations. Your answer to how strongly you identify as a leader is going to depend on your internal expectations of leadership and whether you are living up to your own model of what leadership means to you. This internal definition of leadership is what psychologists term *schemas*, which are developed over time as we learn from the people and events around us. These schemas are hidden and require active self-exploration to unearth.

A delegation of senior managers I recently worked with is a good example. At the beginning of the session, I asked the audience to raise their hand if they saw themselves as a *son* or a *daughter*. As you would expect, each individual put their hand up in recognition of this identity they held. I pointed out, however, that if I were to interview each of them on their interpretation of what being a *son* or a *daughter* meant, a range of different responses would result. On one level there may be commonality around universal themes of love and support; however, there would also be important differences about duty, life choices, culture, and familial expectations. This multiplicity of interpretations is a simple analogy for the role of a leader.

A leader identity approach asks:

- How strongly do you identify as a 'leader'? and

- How would you describe this aspect of who you are?

Testing your identity formation

In this chapter I want to help you to test out where you are on your own journey. From an identity formation perspective, I am interested in the degree to which a leader identity is embedded within your sense of self. Is it something that is well entrenched? Or rather something that feels novel or tenuous, like a new root system taking shape?

Three phases of identity formation

It is helpful to think about the process of forming your leader identity as occurring through three main phases. According to my research, the process can occur from an under-developed leader identity, to a forming leading identity, through to a well-developed and integrated leadership self. This is outlined in Figure 4.2:

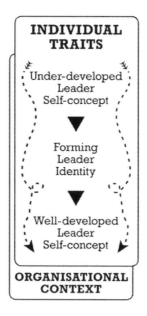

Figure 4.2: Three phases of leader identity formation

Let's cover each of these stages in turn:

Phase 1: Identifying an under-developed leader identity

This is revealed in comments by individuals who don't see themselves as leaders, even when they may be working in a leader-type role. Here's an example of what one of the research participants had to say to this effect:

> "It's funny. I don't see myself as a leader, but I know that lots of people look at me as one."

Typically, individuals at this stage do not yet identify *leader* as a part of who they are. For them being a leader is something that sits outside of their self-definition and belongs to others. In a recent workshop, some of the participants cited self-doubt as a reason they did not identify as leaders. This admission was quite emotional for them and at the same time they expressed relief in being able to acknowledge this. What was important about this discussion was that they were a mix of individuals of different ages, experience, and seniority levels. In other words, their self-doubt and under-developed sense of themselves as leaders brought to life the individuality of leadership and the fact that leadership does not reside with the most senior or experienced among us. Rather, it is something that is open to change, regardless of position or title.

Sometimes individuals with an under-developed leader self-concept recognise a disconnection between their sense of self and the requirements of their role or the views of their colleagues. This was shown in another comment:

> "I don't see myself as a leader. I am paid to be a leader so I better learn how to do it."

I am sure this type of statement is not new to you. You may have heard variations of this from your own colleagues who may dismiss themselves as a 'leader'. Indeed, you may be the one making similar comments – rejecting the idea of seeing yourself this way.

What does this response tell us? And how do you respond to this kind of observation when you hear it or when you are the one feeling it? From a knowing and doing aspect – the traditional responses to developing leaders – the response is to focus on the practice of leadership skills and the gaining of leadership knowledge so that you may learn to become a leader. This knowing and doing approach is valid. There are very real gains that can contribute to becoming a leader and leadership itself represents a lifelong journey of learning.

However, a knowing and doing approach misses the *identity* aspect of leadership and who you already are. If this is the case for you, or someone that you know, it may be fruitful to explore your internal evaluation of leadership – particularly how you may be holding yourself accountable to your own internal leader standard. As you will see in the following chapters, your future development may take the form of raising your awareness of your internal expectations of the role of a 'leader' and helping you to redefine 'leader' more inclusively for yourself.

It is important to note that the apparent disconnect between self-perception (not seeing themselves as leaders) and the perception of others (validating them as leaders) may also be key to their ongoing development and in closing this leadership gap.

For the moment it is important to validate the person's reflection, or your own reflection, and not write it off. It is a significant indicator of the leader identity process that may lie ahead.

Phase 2: Forming leader identity

This phase of identity formation is highlighted by those individuals who recognise themselves as leaders, but are at the same time actively developing aspects of their identity. In other words, they do identify 'leader' within their self-definition; however, they are also actively working through various skills and techniques to consolidate their leadership approach. Psychologists Ely and Rhode refer to this focus on the *doing* of leadership where individuals are consciously trying out various leadership approaches. At the forming stage there is the marked combination of an internal recognition of a leader identity combined with a conscious intention to continue to refine and build it.

In my research, a number of participants were forming their leader identity. One of them reflected on the internal shift that had been taking place, stating:

"I knew I could take on lots of things and I knew I could do things well, but I certainly didn't think that I would be persuasive enough to actually have people want to follow my lead. It's an interesting process of self-discovery."

Another seminar participant reflected on forming their leader identity by highlighting how their recent move to a new department had caused them to reflect on how they were leading in the new context. They had come to the conclusion that whilst they still identified themselves as a leader, they recognised that there were particular skills that needed honing in their new environment. This did not mean a wholesale change in who they were as a leader but rather a refinement of certain aspects of their identity. This combination of recognition of a leader identity, with a focus on particular skill development, is reflective of the forming stage.

Phase 3: Well-developed leader identity

At this other end of the process are those who have a well-formed sense of their leadership self. This is revealed in a confidence and centeredness around who they are as leaders. Their comments often reflect that leadership is another part of their identity, or their way of being in the world. Here's what one participant had to say: "It's just who I am and it's not complicated."

In this phase, individuals have moved to a place of *being* as a leader. This is where the conscious practice that takes place in the forming phase has been replaced by recognition that leadership is a part of their sense of self. This stage was reflected beautifully by one of our clients when she stated that from a very young age she had always identified as a leader. Certain events had undermined this identity in her early twenties, but she was now back in touch with a very deep sense of herself as a leader; so much so that she knew that whatever challenges came her way, she would be able lead her way through.

Exercise 6: Where are you in the formation process?

The scale in Figure 4.3 shows the progression in the early stages of identity formation from a skills or doing focus to a *being* focus where leadership is a part of your identity. Take a moment to rate out of 10 where your leader identity is on this scale (10 being well developed and 1 being underdeveloped). Please note that your self-rating is best captured not by focusing on the role that you are in or whether you lead a team (the hallmarks of the old hierarchical mindset), but rather the degree to which being a leader is a part of you:

Figure 4.3: Identity formation scale

In the space below, write down the reasons why you have rated your leader identity at this level. In your notes, review how comfortable you are with being a leader and/or how intentionally you are trying different skills and techniques. It is important to remember that this self-rating is essential in helping you identify the work you can be doing to continue to form your leader identity and build your career success:

Uncovering your internal leader mindset

The questions below are divided into the identity phases model. Their purpose is to help you identify your leadership mindset, which may be impacting your leader identity formation.

As you will see in the tips below, there are particular developmental areas for you to focus on, depending on where you place yourself on the scale.

Phase 1: Under-developed leader identity

If you consider your leader identity to be underdeveloped, consider these thought starters:

What do you think leadership is? For example: • Does your interpretation of leadership involve big-picture thinking and influence? • Is there a more everyday inclusive definition of leadership that you may apply?	
• In which ways is your definition of leadership tied to seniority or experience? • For example, does it rely on being in a formal leadership role or are you comfortable that individuals can lead from any position – regardless of their title?	
• Are you holding yourself accountable to leadership definitions that are inaccessible?	
• What leadership qualities are you bringing to your role that others can see but you may not?	
• If you don't see yourself as a leader, who are you being in your role? • Where are you having a positive influence?	

Phase 2: Forming leader identity

If you consider yourself to be forming your leader identity, answer the following:

• Which aspects of leading are well-embedded in who you are? • What are you doing when you feel most natural as a leader?	
• Which aspects of your leadership need some attention or development?	
• What steps can you take to showcase your unique leader identity at work or home? • What are your core beliefs around leadership? • What are the principles you stand for and how do you share these with others?	
• Which aspects of leading are unique to you? For example, are you a natural innovator? Or are you a critical thinker? Whatever your innate strengths, these are components of your leader identity and the more frequently you can bring these to life, the more this part of your identity will increasingly feel like a natural part of you.	

Phase 3: Well-developed leader identity

If you do see yourself as a leader, consider these thoughts:

• How are you using your leader identity as a foundation for your career? • Do those around you understand this aspect of who you are?	
• How are you using your leader identity as a foundation for your decision making? As we have seen, the level of ambiguity in our roles will increase in these changing times ahead. As a result, decision making can become more difficult and this is often where our leader identity can be relied upon.	
• How are you acknowledging this aspect of yourself? • Which leader stories do you share? • How often do you share your leadership beliefs, principles, and experiences with those around you?	

Formation is an ongoing process

My research indicates that forming your leader identity is not an afternoon's work but an ongoing process. The old adage that leaders are born and not made did not prevail in my research and simply is not true. Some individuals' life experiences result in a well-developed leader self-concept. However, for others, their identity is less formed or at the very early formation stage, despite their age or experience level. And yet for others they have experienced times when their leader identity was well formed and then times when it has gone through another re-forming process.

These findings reinforce research by psychologists (Dutton, 2010) that identity processes are not once-off events that happen in the early stages of your career development. Rather, identity processes occur over time – often over our entire careers.

A leader identity formation process is an important acknowledgement in recognising the ways in which individuals are constantly refining who they are at work. When we think about who we are and who we are as leaders, this process is one that is never really complete but rather an evolution as we move through life. How has your own leader identity evolved or reformed since your earliest careers days? What kind of leader were you in your first role, and has it reformed since then?

The importance of context

Taking ownership of your leader identity means recognising where you are in the formation process and being active in continuing to develop this aspect of yourself. However, at this juncture we would be very naive if we didn't take into account the influence of your environment on how you may be showing up.

It was the feedback from a sales director that reinforced the ways in which context can impact on formation. The director in question was the eldest, most experienced person in the room. In fact, he beautifully represented the hallmarks of the old paradigm of leadership, where leadership is the domain of the most senior and most knowledgeable among us. Even as an experienced facilitator, I had to keep my assumptions in check as I asked him to rate out of 10 how strongly he identified as a leader (10 being very strong). I was mindful that this was a potentially tricky question to answer in front of his direct reports, particularly where some individuals feel a need to maintain their hierarchical status.

He surprised everyone in the room, including me, when he rated his leader identity at a 3 out of a possible 10. In fact, there were audible gasps from his team as he acknowledged he was at the under-developed end of the scale.

I asked him to explain his self-rating and he went on to illustrate the impact of the industry – his context – on his sense of self. As he told it, two years ago his sense of leadership was very well formed. Back then he was clear about who he was as a leader and what he stood for. He conceded that at that time he would have rated himself a 9 on the identity-formation scale. However, he went on to explain that his leader identity had slowly eroded over recent months as the industry that he worked in changed rapidly. He shared that he found himself scrambling to keep up with the technological advances and at the same time admitted feeling unsure about who he was as a leader within this evolving context. Indeed, it was the conversation around forming and reforming one's leader identity in our seminar that helped him recognise that this was happening.

What a wonderful gift this director gave to himself and to his team. His honesty in sharing where he was in his formation meant he was able to start exploring ways in which he could adapt his leadership self to the changing circumstance. His admission of feeling undermined by the change around him meant that his peers actively voiced their support and encouragement in a way that he needed to hear. Each of his team members expressed they had no inkling and were surprised that this had been a struggle for him, nor had they noticed any shift in his leadership.

What was even more exciting about his *a-ha* moment was that he did it with his team. True to the work of Bene Brown, this leader was unafraid to show his vulnerability and in so doing, he bolstered the trust and respect of his team. After his disclosure, each of his team members felt validated that they could reveal their own struggles and felt able to express these openly. With the honesty and safety established, they were able to look to one another for support in meaningful ways.

This leader's sharing represents a critical aspect of identity formation. As we have seen, it is an ongoing process. However, it is not always in the same direction. The process in becoming a leader is not a linear process from one positive step to the next. Instead, individuals can be undermined in their identity and form and reform them multiple times throughout their career.

Leader identity reformation can be the result of external changes within the environment – highlighting the importance of context. As in this example, context can undermine one's leader identity. It can also reinforce it. The process of forming your leader identity may also change due to internal shifts in your mindset. Either way, the formation process is dynamic in both directions. One's leader identity can be formed and then undermined only to be reformed again, and so on.

This principle was brought to life in a workshop where the organisation was transitioning all its employees out of employment due to a global restructure and an office closure. The managing director spoke about his own leader identity, feeling more uncertain in the face of the uncertainty in the business. This did not mean that he felt he was back in the under-developed stage, but certainly the shifting context had made him rethink his leadership approach and start to form new skills. Interestingly, it was the HR director who spoke about the opposite impact that the transition was having on her leader identity. She mentioned that the requirements of the change called on all her skills, knowledge, and principles as a leader in a way that reinforced or validated her leader identity – regardless of the fact that she would not have a role in six months' time. These counterbalanced responses to the same challenge highlight the way in which one's leader identity is so individually experienced.

The malleable nature of leader identity is not something that is often recognised or discussed. So often we expect that those with the title and the experience are leaders and their leader identity must be cast in stone. We also expect that those without the title are not leaders. Yet, in reality, it may be that those further down the hierarchy have developed their leader identity when those more senior people may be struggling or in the process of reformation. The possibilities of these fluid formation dynamics are endless. At the core of them, however, is the principle that leadership is not done and dusted at an age or a career stage or a salary level. It is an ongoing formation process that can be impacted positively or negatively at any stage or phase.

These conversations resonate with every individual, regardless of their position or title. Thinking about leadership as an ongoing process makes it accessible to everyone. The challenge lies in helping organisations and teams to have the necessary conversations and to tailor the environment so that this level of insight can be validated and supported in a way which increases the leader capability across the company.

Exercise 7: Gaining insight into your context

Understanding yourself and having insight into the organisation you work in is essential for your career success. Whilst forming your leader identity happens throughout your lifetime, being able to see the influences of your work context on your identity will help you to stay true to who you are as a leader.

Research shows that if you are not able to name these dynamics, you run the risk of adopting the problems as something to do with you. Have you ever had the experience of looking back at yourself in a previous role and reflecting that you were not yourself in that job? One reason for this is that, as humans, we can unconsciously internalise the behaviours prevalent in our environment and assume them for ourselves. This may be fine when we are working with a high-performing company and our adoption of new behaviours is part of being successful within that company.

However, this largely unconscious tendency poses a real risk to your identity if you start adopting negative behaviours without realising it. For example, if you happen to be working in a very competitive workplace but do not notice the competition, you may find yourself becoming more competitive than you might otherwise be. If this is left unchecked, it could lead to unintentionally negative behaviour such as becoming territorial or playing unhelpful politics. So, in order to understand who you really are as a leader, you must become better at seeing the cultural/political/power dynamics in your workplace that may be influencing you. Using our tree analogy from earlier – seeing both the forest and the trees.

This insight involves actively describing the cultures within which you work, the forces that shape this culture, and being on the lookout for subtle clues that tell you what is really going on. One of my wonderful colleagues, Kate, is an expert in this area and is able to identify dynamics and norms that so often go unseen and unaddressed. In practice, asking questions such as those suggested below helps you to uncover the hidden dynamics that are a part of every working context. To get started, answer the following questions on your work context:

1. Who has the power in your organisation, division, or team?

2. Who are the decision makers without positional power?

3. What history do the key players have together (if any)? What are the common themes?

4. Which behaviours get rewarded?

5. What is your physical work environment like? For example, are there dedicated areas to commune?

6. What are the pictures/paintings on the walls (if applicable)? What do they tell you about the culture?

Developing this critical insight is key to your career success for two reasons:

- When you have greater contextual insight, you can be active and intentional in the way you decide to handle that environment. In doing so, you increase the likelihood of maintaining your sense of self.

- Naming the hidden trends that you see (recognising that no two cultures are the same) can accelerate your ability to change or influence that workplace. You may wish to move the culture towards one that is inclusive and high performing; however, this may mean being prepared to address unhelpful dynamics.

Leader formation through transitions

Any type of career transition presents the risk of undermining your sense of who you are and how you are showing up. If left unchecked, transitions can have a very real impact on your identity formation. You may be working towards a new role, setting up a new business, or returning to work following parental leave. Whilst each of these transitions is relatively common, our ability to understand their potential impact on our identity formation is not so common.

To understand the potential impact of transitions, we need to understand the impact that a change in circumstance can have on our sense of self. As we have seen earlier, we are all products of our environment to some extent and we have elements of our identity tied to these various environments. At work we may be the successful people manager, at home the reliable parent, with our peers the confident mentor, and on the tennis court the competitive sportsperson. Each of these selves make up our identity. When looking at the transitions people experience when taking on new jobs or changing careers or moving towards retirement, it is important to understand that these times often provide individuals with opportunities for renegotiating both their private and public views of their leader identity. That is the way they look at themselves and the opportunities they see for their future.

Moving away from old roles can be a time for testing out a new way of being – out of the comfort zone of what is known and towards a new aspect of your identity. Small and sometimes large shifts in individual identities can take place through transition. Similarly, in times of transition, changes can occur for individuals in their anticipated future career ideas, marriage, parenthood, health, and lifestyle areas at the same time. This was particularly relevant for a client who was transitioning from a local to a global role with her organisation. At one level in her coaching program, the work was focused on the transactional nature of the transition – the new team, new environment, culture, and everyday changes to her context. Yet on a far deeper level was the fact that she was gradually updating her own sense of identity and who she was as a leader. She would be the first to say that the first six months of her transition had moments of great self-doubt; however, throughout the time, she also knew she could rely on her deeply held beliefs, principles, and values to be successful.

One mechanism for understanding these potential identity changes – whether they represent subtle shifts for the person or are transformational in nature – is the theory of possible selves. The concept of possible selves was first developed by psychologists Hazel Markus and Paula Nurius who introduced it to complement the thinking around understanding our inner selves and how we build and shape our identities over our lifetime. They noted that "possible selves represent an individual's ideas of what they might become, what they would like to become, and what they are afraid of becoming" in the future. They highlighted that possible selves are the images, senses, and thoughts that individuals carry around in their heads and are dependent on that individuals' personal history, motives, experiences, values, and beliefs.

As such, possible future selves represent the specific and individual hopes, fears, and dreams of each person. "I am now a customer service manager but could be a restaurant owner, a marathon runner, or a journalist" are all examples of possible selves that are highly individualised and personalised.

The concept highlights that an individual is free to create any variety of possible selves, yet the pool of possible selves that are created are wholly dependent on that person's history, culture, social interactions, and individual background. Barrack Obama's successful move to president of the United States has no doubt influenced and opened up the idea of this future possible self for many Americans of varying ethnicity. Similarly, it could be said that Australia's first female Governor General, Quentin Bryce, fostered the creation of a new possible self – a political/cultural leader possible self for many Australian women.

On a smaller scale, possible selves can help us make sense of all the different roles in our life that make up our identity and that we are trying to hold together. The juggle for new mothers who want to balance their work possible selves with their parenting possible selves is a classic example. Similarly, juggling new leadership roles or taking on new business opportunities or choosing to work flexibly are all examples of these different life choices. Importantly, each individual's choice will be wholly dependent on their background, goals, and workplace choices and are highly individualised.

Markus and Nurius highlighted that desired future possible selves "stand as symbols of hope". They also highlighted that future selves that are negative "are reminders of sad figures that are to be avoided". Importantly, however, the concept is helpful given that "all of these ideas about what is possible for us to be, to think, to feel, or to experience provide a direction and impetus for action, change, and development". It is in this context that the notion of possible selves can be linked to our own motivation. Specifically, possible selves can help guide behaviour and action toward what we want to become (the leader selves we hope for) and away from undesired outcomes (our feared selves).

Importantly, the concept of possible selves is one that recognises that these selves can change on a regular basis and are highly reliant on changes in circumstances/opportunities, resources, and constraints. The possible leader selves that we held for ourselves in our 20s are likely to be quite different to the possible selves that we find ourselves navigating today. This is not to say that we have moved away from our authentic selves (or at least hopefully we haven't) but rather that our inner hopes and fears have persisted over time but have also been adapted to our current situations.

In managing our leader formation, possible selves are useful in helping us to map out and play around with what it is that we would like, may like, or could make happen for our future. In mapping these out, we can begin to understand the first steps of how to get there.

Exercise 8: Possible selves

1. What is the main leader identity or possible self that you see for your future?

2. Which values of yours does this support?

3. What are your hopes and fears for this possible self?

4. How likely is it that this possible self could transpire?

5. How motivating is this possible self to you? Circle your answer, where: 10 = high and 1 = low.

    1   2   3   4   5   6   7   8   9   10

6. What actions can you take to explore this further?

    i.

    ii

    iii.

A fundamental premise of career *progression* is to constantly build and refine your leader identity; a key aspect of your self-awareness. In fact, this is the foundation for showcasing and articulating your values, morals, beliefs, and experiences. However, this identity awareness can be lost without an ongoing and increasing capacity to understand the unique organisational context in which you find yourself. Wherever you may be in the formation process of your leader identity, it is critical that you spend time reflecting on this aspect of yourself. This is because you may face very real detractors and obstacles that can pull you from your leadership identity or undermine your formation process. Being active in noticing your environment will equip you to manage these factors. It will also increase the likelihood that you can realise your leadership self at work.

Finally, whether you are transitioning your leader identity or not, give yourself the freedom to say yes to the opportunities that come your way. Seize them. Invest in them and yourself. Choose to be decisive about the direction you want to take and the leader you want to be.

This journey towards stepping into your leadership potential is a process that can lift your personal satisfaction and contribute to greater career longevity. My approach to helping you do this in a sustainable way, supported by my research findings, is to tackle this in two ways:

- By strengthening your leader identity; and

- Protecting it from being undermined.

These areas form the focus of the next chapters.

Chapter 5

Self-strategies to strengthen your leader identity

Helping you strengthen your leader identity is critical to your ongoing success and wellbeing. Strengthening your identity means taking into account the dynamic nature of your sense of self and the fact that it may be reinforced, or undermined, depending on what is happening in your life. Given this changeability, this chapter is based on the principle that it is not enough that you may see yourself as a leader unless you are active in strengthening and protecting this part of who you are. This combined perspective is reflected in Figure 5.1.

A series of enabling factors were identified in my research to help accelerate or strengthen the formation of one's leader identity. These enablers are internal (to the self) and external (relating to each individual's environment). As we have seen, individuals typically navigate their own formation path; however, there are several universal techniques that can be applied to progress it.

In my research there were four *internally* focused strategies you can pursue to strengthen your leader identity. Each of these strategies are supported in the wider research literature as evidence-based strategies to assist your development:

1. Personalising leadership
2. Achieving authenticity
3. Being change-ready
4. Adopting an inclusive mindset

This chapter is dedicated to the first two internal strategies, or what I term self-strategies: **personalising leadership** and **achieving authenticity**.

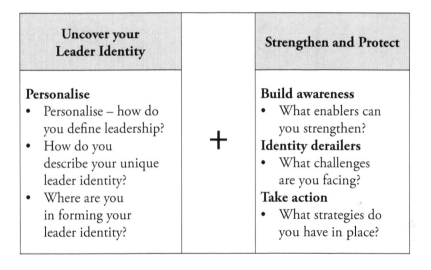

Uncover your Leader Identity		Strengthen and Protect
Personalise • Personalise – how do you define leadership? • How do you describe your unique leader identity? • Where are you in forming your leader identity?	**+**	**Build awareness** • What enablers can you strengthen? **Identity derailers** • What challenges are you facing? **Take action** • What strategies do you have in place?

Figure 5.1: Uncovering and strengthening your leader identity

Personalising leadership

Personalising leadership means defining leadership on your own terms, as I have stated numerous times in the preceding chapters. You may recall that this is a core principle of this guide and is a key hallmark of successful individuals. High performers define leadership in ways that are meaningful to them and their environment. They notice the norms that prevail, they are insightful into the dynamics around them, and they take ownership of their own leadership approach. Importantly too, they are not afraid to stand up for what they believe in, and it is this bedrock that they rely on in their work. As a result, research shows they enjoy career promotion, success, and longevity.

The exercises you have done so far in Chapters 3 and 4 have started this personalising process for you. However, it would be unrealistic to claim that having read this guide you will come out with a completed account of your leader identity. What is realistic is that as you continue reading, you will have more insight into who you are as a leader. All of these exercises are designed to motivate you to continue to define and refine how you intend to make a positive difference to those around you and personalise leadership in your own way.

To give you a sense of what personalising leadership means, I encourage you to chat with people in your life about what leadership means to them. This is an important active listening exercise because it requires you to pay attention to individual perspectives on leadership that each person has. I can guarantee you that if you ask five different people what leadership means to them or how they lead, you will receive five different answers. Here are two very concise leader identities from workshop participants:

Participant 1: Innovative, creative, persistent

Participant 2: Generosity, giving back, mentoring

Exercise 9: Interviewing stakeholders

Asking leaders who are embedded in the command and control version of leadership to articulate their approach is fascinating. However, you must exhibit caution and respect in these conversations, as I am sure you do in every such conversation. Each person's interpretation of leadership is extremely personal –

built up over their lifetimes and influenced by their personal life events. So, if you receive a "lead from the front, set the vision, be the one in charge" response, then at the very least you know what to expect from that individual.

In these exploratory conversations, it is imperative that you do not bring your own biases to the table. For example, a command and control leadership style has merit in some contexts. It is also important to recognise that many of those embedded in a command paradigm often wish they didn't have to bear the brunt of the decisions. In coaching conversations, these clients are often willing to recognise that they need to let go of the old mindset and make a change. Many of them are exhausted at feeling the need to be in control and many have been subconsciously looking for a better way, or certainly feeling a deep sense of dissatisfaction. Similarly, from a development perspective, I am sure you can point to a time in your life when the command and control model was the foundation of your own approach; particularly as humans have the tendency to internalise the behaviours and norms of the people around us. And for many years, command and control has been the norm.

However, perhaps far more importantly, this feedback gives you a rich insight into their mindset and, if managed well, the opportunity to explore their approach. You may choose to interview this person so that you can both reach a greater mutual understanding of what it means to lead. Or you may choose to open up this dialogue with them to help change their thinking. Either way, exploring the interpretation of leadership with the people whom you work with, or significant others in your life, is an important opportunity. This is because it is a topic that very rarely gets discussed, yet has such a fundamental impact on their life and the lives of those around them, including you. Of course this type of dialogue is easily translatable to job interviews, the start of new projects, and any other setting where you need to meet with people.

Consider the last time you were part of a cross-functional team. How did you know what to expect from one another or how best to work with them? How long did it take to work this out? What if you could have short-cut this process? How would that have impacted you or the project's performance? Imagine if each team member was able to address this upfront. Perhaps it would sound a little like this:

> "I would really like us to take a minute each to understand how we all prefer to work and what leadership means to each of us. From my perspective, you will get the best out of me if I can bring plenty of structure to the project. I am a very planful leader and I believe no detail is too small. Leadership to me is about providing clear pathways to achieve the project's vision. I am a really organised person and you can count on me to contribute, particularly when I can input into our direction and planning."

Or this:

> "I'm not sure what to expect from this project team, but I can let you know I am a very entrepreneurial thinker. Being creative and challenging the status quo is part of who I am. As a leader, you can expect me to be honest, candid, and to ask plenty of questions. Just because we have always done it that way is not a reason to keep doing it, so you can rely on me to mix things up a bit. So now that I have shared, perhaps we can go around the group and get everyone to talk about their take on what leading means and who they are."

Stakeholder interview questions

If you choose to interview key people or stakeholders on what leadership means to them, the following questions can be useful:

1. How would you describe your approach to leading?

2. Where does it come from? What life events have shaped this?

3. Who were the main influences in your approach? Which aspects of their leadership did you like and/or emulate?

4. Are there aspects of your leadership that you have adapted over time? How much of your approach is still open to change?

5. How does your approach marry with the idea of empowering everyone to lead?

Many years ago, one of my first coaching clients was a C-level executive in one of Australia's largest financial institutions. He was from South Africa and as part of his citizenship, he had spent a few formative years in the army. The probability that the sessions would be embedded in a command and control mindset was expected from the outset. And yet, of course, it didn't turn out that way. Instead, he was a leader who relied on humility, common sense, and a deep commitment to living his values. To every meeting he carried a fairly worn manila folder in which he had pasted various quotes, pictures, and visual images to remind him of what he stood for. He told me that every time he was about to enter a particularly stressful meeting (which at his level was often), he took a couple of minutes to read through them. This simple practice ensured he remained grounded and true to his leadership self. The folder effectively and beautifully captured his unique leader identity.

There are so many aspects of this story that I love, but one is that he was so transparent about how he used the folder. He was forthright about how much it helped him to show up in a way he was proud of. The simple act of re-reading aspects of his identity – which in reality took only moments to do – gave him the inner awareness and clarity to make the best decisions and to be true to himself. I also love the fact that as the head of IT in the finance company, he could have had any range of wildly technological ways to build his folder, yet he chose to do it in the most basic, practical way. I take a lot from this example because this is exactly what I have chosen to do with this guide – to bring it back to the basics and provide you with straightforward yet effective ways to build and refine your leader identity.

Achieving authenticity

If individuals are unclear about their leader identity, what impact does this have on their overall effectiveness?

Authentic leaders are defined as having a deep sense of self and being clear about their values and beliefs. The term refers to knowing your core values, beliefs, and principles, as well as your unique talents, strengths, and your desires and goals. Authenticity also includes having a basic fundamental awareness of your knowledge, experience, and capabilities. The concept of authenticity goes back to ancient Greek philosophy with the adage "to thine own self be true". Psychologists Bruce Avolio and William Gardner added to this definition by including "your cognitions regarding your identity" – in our language this means knowing who you are and who you are as a leader. One research participant captured the essence of achieving authenticity, stating that it was:

"… remaining true to who you are, to your ethics, and your values. Not going, 'Okay, I'm surrounded by a culture that doesn't really work for me' and stepping over the line into becoming that."

Researchers actually disagree more than they agree on all of the components that make someone authentic. However, many of the authentic leadership models such as Transformational Leadership, Charismatic Leadership, Servant Leadership, and Spiritual Leadership do agree on one aspect – self-awareness. Indeed, self-awareness is seen as the building block of authenticity.

According to Avolio and his team, authentic leaders are thought to be transparent in their decision making and share their thought processes with their relevant stakeholders. They seek differing inputs and perspectives as part of their everyday work rather than relying on the same sources of information. The researchers termed this *balanced processing*, which refers to leaders who show they go through a due diligence to objectively analyse all relevant data before coming to a decision. This includes soliciting views that challenge their deeply held positions prior to making important decisions, in order to be seen as fair and just. The diversity and transparency that form part of these behaviours in balanced processing are particularly relevant for building trust in your leadership. Being able to clearly articulate who you are as a leader, what leadership means to you, and translating this into behaviours that your peers/team/colleagues can expect from you, is immensely powerful. This communication showcases the ownership you have taken of your leader identity and also sends a clear message to your colleagues. What a fabulous foundation for mutual trust!

Self-awareness

Self-awareness is always the starting point for achieving authenticity. How can you learn to connect with others better if you do not understand yourself? How can you be true to your leader identity if you have no insight into your unique characteristics?

Consider some of these simple self-awareness questions:

- Do you know how you feel and can you truthfully assess your emotions? For example: "I can't seem to concentrate and I don't know why" vs "I feel anxious at the moment like I do every time I'm about to present".

- Are you able to label your emotions and own them rather than blame them on someone or something else? For example: "I feel frustrated" vs "My work never gives me what I need".

- Can you talk about what you are feeling and reflect on this? For example: "I feel really energised today and I know it's because I really like solving problems in this job."

- Are you able to make the link between what you are feeling and how that may be affecting your performance? For example: "When I am motivated, I am really focused and far more efficient."

- Can you accurately list your strongest capabilities and where you need development? For example: "My client relationship skills are really strong, but I know I need help when it comes to standing my ground during conflict."

These questions are all part of your emotional intelligence (EI). One key result of high EI is the ability to encourage positive outcomes in others. By this I mean the ability to read the reactions of people that you deal with and consciously manage your own communication so that you may get a better outcome. Managing emotions and recognising these emotions are hallmarks of high EI individuals. Skills such as developing others, influencing, and conflict management are all part of relationship management. They all depend on your self-awareness and your awareness of yourself as a leader.

Interestingly, your ability to accurately assess yourself and your talents is a sign of high self-awareness and has been shown as the key characteristic of superior performance. In fact, average performers tend to overestimate their strengths, whereas top performers rarely do. Which one are you?

I attended a session by Daniel Goleman, the most cited author of emotional intelligence, at the Institute of Coaching conference in 2014. Having used the EI framework for many years in my work, it stood out for me that embedded within EI is the assumption that people with high EI see themselves as leaders. Goleman didn't focus on this attribute in this session; however, in our leader identity perspective, it is hugely important. It is important because it raises the question: Does high EI provide the insight for people to see themselves as leaders? If so, does building more leaders equate to building the emotional intelligence of individuals? In other words, are you best served, after reading this guide, to actively build your EI? Or is it that those people who see themselves as leaders already have high EI? Have they been able to take ownership of their own identity in a way that facilitates a higher level of emotional intelligence? We can't answer these questions here; however, they do raise some interesting questions for further exploration. However, I do think it is safe to conclude that building insight into your own emotions and the emotions of others will assist in building your leader identity.

There are many tools available to assist you in understanding your own levels of EI. I particularly like the Mayer–Salovey–Caruso Emotional Intelligence Test (MSCEIT) because it actually tests your ability to recognise, use, understand, and manage emotions in yourself and others, rather than trying to describe this part of who you are.

Insight into your emotional inner life and the life of others is one way to build your leader authenticity. Indeed, understanding the significant value and influence that you as an individual can have is often a powerful realisation. For others to really appreciate you and to see the benefits of your ideas, they need to know who you are.

Challenges

Achieving authenticity in leadership sounds easier than it is. This is particularly true when we acknowledge that we are all influenced by the people and cultures around us. These environmental influences, organisational norms, as well as the beliefs that we internalise, can be barriers to showing up as our authentic selves. One example comes from a global organisation I have been working with that is both highly successful and highly competitive. Individuals working within the organisation run the risk of amplifying this organisational norm by adopting more competitive stances with one another – potentially to the detriment of team productivity, let alone their own sense of self. Achieving authenticity in this particular organisation requires insight into this dynamic and intentionally navigating the culture from a place of continual self-awareness.

A first checkpoint in understanding how authentic you are at work and as a leader is to consider the following question:

> Can you put your hand on your heart and say that who you are at work is the same as who you are outside of work?

Before we go further, let me clarify this point. I am not suggesting that you are absolutely yourself at work as you are at home. I am sure there is wriggle room for how you deal with your team members versus your family members, friends, and so on. There are very real professional standards that are at play in our workplaces and these need to be adhered to. Professionalism and behaving appropriately and respectfully are foundations of work. However, these standards shouldn't prevent you from being you – put another way, there is you at home and there is you at work; however, it is all the same you.

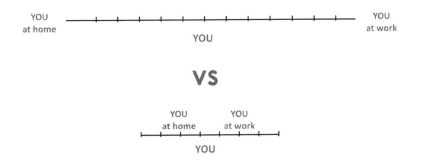

Figure 5.2: Differing degrees of authenticity

The key to being more authentic at work lies in being able to draw the two versions of who you are closer together as highlighted by the bottom line in Figure 5.2. Professionalism is a foundation for leadership and this can account for the slight variance in how you show up. In other words, there are very real reasons to be more formal or more restrained in certain work settings. However, it is vitally important to your wellbeing to work in ways which draw upon your innate strengths and showcase who you really are. This alignment is even more important to your authenticity as a leader. One client mentioned how humour came naturally to him. However, in a professional setting he has learnt to rein it in appropriately. As a leader, a foundation of his identity is grounded in this lightness; however, he also has enough awareness to know when it can be unhelpful to the people around him.

Individuals who report a significant difference between who they are at work and who they are at home – shown in the top line of Figure 5.2 – can often suffer energy depletion as they try to manage this incongruence. In worst-case scenarios this can lead to burnout and even opting out of the workforce; particularly when they have no awareness of this difference. Over the years my colleagues and I have worked with numerous clients who have recognised that they are not being true to themselves at work. Often, but not always, this is due to a fear that they may be penalised in some way for not conforming to the dominant norms within their organisations. The self-censorship that can result then becomes both exhausting and self-defeating for them. Instead, their coaching work becomes navigating these expectations and bringing more of their talents, strengths, and principles to their role. In every situation there is always opportunity to be more authentic. The secret is often in taking the time to reflect and do the hard work of analysing how you are showing up.

Achieving authenticity can also be a minefield in terms of the culture within which you work and the dominant language of your company. Let me give you an example. As part of an introduction to a recent leadership conference, I decided to give the audience two stories – one was about my drive to achieve and the things I have done in my career nationally and internationally. The second was about overcoming adversity with my health and feeling like I am finally winning by getting this back on track. Both stories were achievement oriented but very different in nature – one more about the facts and data, the other far more personal.

Where authenticity becomes a potential minefield is because, for some of the audience, the story of achievements would have resonated. Some of them may have been particularly data driven or that may be their preferred communication style. Give them the facts and they are satisfied. Yet, for others in the audience, the health story may have been more interesting given their preference for more interpersonal communication and getting to know the personal aspects of someone. These communication preferences are an important difference that can confound perceptions of authenticity.

Then we need to overlay these communication preferences with each individual's views on leadership. My data-driven story may have alienated those who may have held a preference that women leaders shouldn't be too assertive or talk about their achievements, so I may have been penalised in their minds. On the flipside, some members of the audience may have thought that my personal health story was too personal, a sign of weakness, and that women leaders should be more professional and maintain their boundaries. So, I may have been penalised by them too. This is just one example of the 'double bind' that many women may face when it comes to being an authentic woman leader. Alice Eagly (2005) called this relational authenticity; meaning that the people around you need to validate your authentic leadership and/or your values and see you as a legitimate leader. Context is key and helping individuals with insight into this judgement – to see the individual, not the gender – is part of the work we all still need to do. It is also something that can get in the way of achieving authenticity.

Strengths

From a leader identity perspective, being familiar with the innate strengths you bring to your career and being active in living these, is critical in building trust with those around you. As we have said, authentic leaders are those who understand who they are and are grounded in their own sense of self. They are not afraid to be themselves and their consistency builds safety and trust in the people around them.

The wonderful thing about strengths is that they exist in every individual, much like the capacity to lead. Strengths represent parts of your character and come naturally to you. In fact, when you are operating in your strengths, you experience greater meaning and energy. There is now a vast amount of research which shows that individuals who get to use their strengths more frequently are also happier, more confident, more resilient, and experience less stress.

Strengths are also relatively easy to identify. Typically, situations where you are feeling most energised or engaged signal that your strengths may be activated. Some clients reflect that this is when they are in dialogue with clients, building relationships. Others reflect that it is when they are deep into a spreadsheet, solving complex problems. For others it may be when they are creating artwork, and so on.

The important message is that working with your own strengths builds your mood and motivation. This is largely because research has shown that when you are activating your strengths, you are also building your positive emotions. Strengths are inherently satisfying. In the burgeoning area of positive psychology, we know that positive emotions increase your ability to think and to be creative and innovative. In other words, utilising your strengths builds your positive emotions which broaden your mindset and allow you to think in new and exciting ways. This building of positive emotions leads to an upward spiral in performance through improved practices and better coping skills.

Thanks to the work of Dr Barbara Fredrickson, we know that there exists a positivity ratio for positive and negative emotions that can lead to increased motivation. Her extensive research showed that if an individual or team experience meets the 3 to 1 ratio – three positive emotions to one negative – team motivation and morale are enhanced. A side note is that the three emotions do not need to be due to praise only. Instead, they could result from communication styles that create positive emotion. For example, it may be that your communication is based on inquiry rather than telling. This is because asking questions rather than advocating your position reflects a simple strategy that can build the positive emotion in any dialogue.

If you are unsure about your innate strengths or the values that are important to you, I recommend accessing some of the online surveys that are available. In our programs we currently choose to use the VIA Strengths Survey (www.viacharacter.org) and there is a short online version that you can do free of charge. Once you have done this, or any other tool that appeals to you, the insight comes in taking the time to translate your strengths into describing your leader identity. This involves using language that helps people understand you better. Here is an example from a recent client:

"As a leader I am passionate about delivering results. Continuous improvement and perseverance are some of my signature strengths. Helping organisations streamline their work and build efficiencies is a principal that I hold deeply."

Working to your strengths is something we can all continue to enhance. This is particularly relevant when you consider the various domains of your life – work, home, friendships, relationships, and so on. These different life areas present a great opportunity to think about how you can express your natural strengths more frequently. One woman reported that being very honest in her workplace is something that comes easy to her as it is one of her top strengths and reflects the cultural norms of her company. Yet she conceded that she was less honest in her personal life and found suppressing this natural strength disconcerting. Her area for development became finding scenarios with her significant others where she could express her honesty in a confident way. Another client reflected that, as a father, he was very loving in his family life and with his friends. Again, this came naturally to him as it was one of his signature strengths. However, he recognised that he played down this aspect of his character in his work environment for fear of being judged. His development became finding ways to integrate his nurturing self into his work.

The overuse of strengths is one aspect to be cautious of. Whilst high performers have a good awareness of their strengths, they are also cognisant of where these default strengths can undermine their communication. For example, leaders with high humility can become unstuck in cultures of self-promotion and not position themselves well in these environments. Similarly, a natural strength of kindness can be overdone and undermine performance discussions. Again, relying on one's default strength of honesty can undermine relationships and do more harm in certain contexts. One client was very popular with his peers and was often seen as the 'go-to' person whenever there was a crisis in the office. His dilemma was dealing with all of the unplanned interruptions that this natural strength would cause. Coaching revealed that he was very good at listening to the woes of his four daughters, therefore he was quite adept at playing to this strength with his peers. The only problem was that it was getting in the way of his productivity. The solution? Rather than just being 'the ear' of the work team and valuing his strength in building relationships, he began to introduce more of his other strengths to the group. This meant he drew from his strength in honesty and remained kind with his peers, but firmer, with clearer expectations being set. He outlined that he was happy to listen, but only if the conversation resulted in an action from the peer to resolve the issue – not unlike managing the challenges of his daughters. Being able to recognise what your natural strengths are and how you can draw on them in concert with your other strengths – like relationships and honesty in this example – is an important key to achieving authenticity.

The ideal goal of working with your strengths is to rely on the right strengths, to the right degree, in the right context. From a leader identity perspective, concentrating on conveying your strengths will add to your satisfaction and motivation.

A good listener – whether they are your manager, peer, friend, or coach – is able to listen out for strengths. This concept of strengths spotting is a wonderful perspective that is gaining ground in many organisations. It refers to the simple act of identifying and naming the strengths you see in others. In team environments, morale increases when peers take the time and make an effort to reflect on the strengths they see in others. This simple exercise is validating for the receiver but also validating for the giver. Many great leaders pride themselves on being able to identify the strengths in others and tailor their feedback to these strengths. There is a lot of work going on in organisations asking individuals to shape their own work roles in a way that plays to their strengths. This is a far more powerful approach as research shows that focusing on strengths leads to greater performance versus the traditional approach of rectifying weaknesses.

The concept of collective strengths in teams is a wonderful way to improve engagement and results. When a strengths approach is taken at a team level and actively reinforced by the members, research shows that team performance and engagement increase significantly. These strengths exercises create a unified dialogue for teams and help team members understand one another better. Some organisations have used collective strengths to divide work tasks more appropriately and match the task to the strength. In asking team members which tasks they feel most aligned to, teams report an increase in creativity, problem solving, and collaboration. Many teams reflect that strengths discussions allow leaders to emerge organically and remove hierarchical limits by validating the strengths in everyone.

Principles

Achieving authenticity as a leader is also about being clear about the principles you stand for. These are the experiences and beliefs that have shaped you and form a part of your leader identity. These are more than the characteristics you value or the strengths that are part of you. These principles reflect your various life events. You may have a particular principle centred on generosity and giving back. You may consider that loyalty is a foundation of who you are. Being able to tell your stories and share the aspects of leadership that have shaped you is fundamental to building relationships with the people around you and achieving authenticity in leadership.

In conveying your principles, I am reminded of a client who shared her story with her team. She told them of her impoverished childhood in South America. She began working at the age of 6, helping her parents sell their produce at local markets. Sometimes she was the only one at the stall and this responsibility weighed heavily on her. Today she reflects on the powerful principles she learnt from these experiences. She tells of how, in having to mature early, she also built her confidence in connecting with people older than her and negotiating with them on an even level. She also learnt that no job was worth doing unless you were going to give 100% every time. These principles of equality in negotiation, and bringing your best self to the job, are expectations she holds for her team today. These principles serve as pillars for her team and help guide them in delivering their top results.

I can't raise the concept of principles without mentioning another wonderful colleague, Sheba. Sheba is a leadership coach based in Delhi and her principles of inclusion and compassion are at the forefront of her leader identity. Working with Sheba and watching her facilitate is a privilege. This is because her principles ground every aspect of her approach. She applies them to her work in such a way that she promotes an environment of safety and kindness that has a spiritual essence to it. More importantly it compellingly engages her audience and opens them to new possibilities.

Exercise 10: Creating your leader stories

The following exercise is designed to help you identify a principle and relevant life story that starts to capture what you stand for as a leader. Consider the key elements and write down one example that comes to mind for you:

BACKGROUND: What was the background of the scene? (Who, what, where)

OPPORTUNITY: What was the challenge you faced?

SOLUTION: How did you solve it?

SIGNIFICANCE: Which of your leadership characteristics did you draw upon?

By completing a sample of leadership stories that showcases you as a leader, you will be far more prepared to explain to your colleagues, team, and stakeholders not only who you are as a leader but also what they can expect from you. This is a critical aspect of leading; allowing you to be both transparent and consistent in your leadership endeavours. The power of your stories lies in helping you determine the aspects of leadership that are most meaningful to you, showcasing the often hidden expectations of yourself and others. Storytelling itself is a developmental activity because it forces you to think more deeply about aspects of your identity and it forms your views of and experiences with others.

If you ever have the opportunity to share stories with others, I encourage you to relish it. This is such a wonderful chance to compare your similarities, notice your differences, and connect more deeply. Every time these stories are told in our sessions, there is laughter, joy, tears, and admiration. It seems that in encouraging individuals to tell their leader stories, we get to witness the incredible preciousness of each person at their best. Fundamentally, when this is occurring, you are relating your experiences, presenting them to others, sometimes analysing them for the first time, and finally taking action because of them.

These stories do not always need to be positive either. One client spoke of his experience growing up in a low socio-economic area and learning to keep his head down to avoid retribution. He recognised that he didn't put himself forward at work due to this long-held fear. However, through his storytelling he realised that this belief was one that he could now let go of. In his own words, he stated, "I realise today there would be no one at the end of the driveway getting ready to knock me down!"

Corporate storytelling is an activity that is very popular because organisations that use it recognise its power to communicate a message, set the right context, and wrap up the past. This activity is just as powerful at an individual level.

Exercise 11: Authenticity checklist

Your willingness to share your insights, values, and natural strengths is a powerful way to build your authenticity and to be heard. The following questions are a useful checklist to help you identify areas to continue achieving authenticity:

1. Are people clear about your views and what you stand for?

2. What are your top 3 to 5 principles/beliefs or values that you can list right here and now?

3. Do you state your position clearly and link the reasons for your position to your values or beliefs? For example: "This is very important to me because ..."

4. How can you be more open about your feelings, taking ownership of who you are, and share these with others? For example: "I feel disappointed because ..."

And finally, trying to be consistent with using your strengths and values is not an easy task. However, in attempting to do this, you become an authentic role model for others.

Here's an example from a client of forming parts of his leader identity:

As a young man this client always forgave his friends when they left the friendship group to be with their girlfriends, only to return later once the relationship was over. Instead of judging the friends for their actions, this client was always the voice of understanding. In his words, he learnt from these early experiences that in being there for others, they would be there for him. He says this spirit of reciprocity is a strength that underpins his leadership today and has enabled him to forge lifelong relationships.

Chapter 6

Further self-strategies to strengthen your leader identity

This chapter is dedicated to the two additional self-strategies to strengthen your leader identity which were uncovered in my research: **Being change-ready** and **adopting an inclusive mindset**.

Being change-ready

Defining leadership on your own terms does not mean that you define it to the exclusion of feedback from others. Instead, your identity is a platform for your career that must always be open to adaptation. If self-awareness is the first step toward achieving authenticity and strengthening your leader identity, then your adaptability is the second. This openness to change asks you to consider the ways in which you shape your environment by being true to yourself and the ways in which you are *shaped by* your environment through the feedback of others. Adaptability of your leader identity or being change-ready is the second key characteristic for career success.

I have spent a lot of time in this guide asking you to reflect on the aspects of your past that have shaped your ideas on leadership and on who you are as a leader. However, this chapter refers to a future focus. It refers to the degree to which you are willing to embrace change and remain open-minded. Leaders with a good sense of who they are in the world are paradoxically also open to changing, to learning, and to adapting.

Being open-minded and constantly adapting or updating your leader identity is central to strengthening your leader identity. In our seminars, some attendees find embracing these two potentially conflicting perspectives difficult. There is a natural tension between maintaining your authentic leader identity on the one hand, and on the other hand openly adapting your perspectives, behaviours, and skills, as seen in Figure 6.1:

Figure 6.1: Managing consistency and adaptation

Navigating this natural tension is inherent in the approach of successful leaders. Research by Herminia Ibarra into the strategies of lawyers seeking promotion suggested that those who remained true to their sense of self, without adapting their behaviours, were less likely to be promoted. Instead, the individuals who were promoted had recognised the need to adapt their behaviours to their environment, and they had managed to do this without sacrificing their core leader identity.

Openness to change is fundamental to continuing to progress in your career because if you are open to change, you are open to improve. It is particularly relevant as you come across new experiences or situations that may require a refinement of your skills or attitudes in order to meet the needs of the new environment. A failure to recognise the need for change can result in failure more generally. Consider this: I recently had a client who had spent most of her career being the driver of change for her organisation. She managed the projects, she headed the steering committee, and she ultimately took responsibility for the delivery of the team's results. Her leader identity was grounded in being the innovator, being process oriented, and being a change agent. Paradoxically, her difficulties arose when her organisation was bought by a much larger one. In the merged environment, she faced passive resistance and an unwillingness of the new stakeholders to take action.

After many sleepless nights trying to understand why, she realised that it was her own default approach – her passion for change – that was getting in her way. The merger required that a whole new set of behaviours needed to be adapted into her leadership repertoire. This included practising skills such as exploratory dialogue and political savvy. This needed to be mixed with a heavy dose of patience before she could even begin a change process. Her insight into her leader identity and her changing circumstance was aided by her attendance at our program and the ability to reflect with an objective listener on what was going on. Importantly, her realisation did not undermine her leader identity because she was able to recognise her authentic self – the change maker – and adapt it to the new circumstance in an empowered way. Wouldn't we all have liked this realisation in similar circumstances? How many careers could have been aided by this insight?

As we have seen in the changing context of our world, being prepared to change and to experience discomfort through making change, is required now more than ever before. The client in the previous example did not find the changes easy – far from it. She was often frustrated and upset at how she needed to manage herself and the situation. However, she was open to feeling the discomfort. She understood that by putting herself through it, she would gain even more insights into herself and navigate her environment more successfully. So, the situation got difficult but her openness to change meant that she stayed engaged and persevered.

Being prepared to take action and to continue your development in an open-minded way will assist you in achieving your goals. However, not everyone is comfortable with this. From a developmental perspective, there are many individuals who would prefer to stay true to their own sense of self than to change. In fact, they are probably the majority, not the norm. However, that mindset is a recipe for potential failure. Certainly, if you are in an environment that remains static, then you have a greater chance of not coming undone. However, if, like me, you live in a world full of new ideas and new approaches, then you cannot afford to ignore the forest for the trees. From a leader identity perspective, openness to change is a key characteristic of successful leaders; particularly as situations evolve and the requirement to adapt one's leadership approach in an intentional way becomes more relevant.

Herminia Ibarra's book, *Act like a Leader, Think like a Leader,* highlights this. She says act first and *then* change your way of thinking. As opposed to insight, she calls acting differently enhancing your 'outsight'. In other words, by choosing to act differently in a situation, you will change the way you think about yourself as a leader. I like this terminology because it can help us get unstuck. When you think about areas in your life that need changing, perhaps the first step is in making a step towards the change and then reflecting on it.

From a team perspective, the concept of embracing change is captured beautifully in a book by Amy Edmonson (2012), *Teaming – How Organisations Learn, Innovate and Compete in the Knowledge Economy.* In this comprehensive review of the impact of change on team dynamics, four principles recommended by Amy stand out:

1. Aim high. In an era of constant change, teams need to be more aspirational and reinforce their purpose.

2. Team up. The complexity of work means that successful teams work across borders and functions to integrate diverse perspectives.

3. Fail well. Anticipating and mitigating failure and, most importantly, building active reflection into team processes is an important routine to establish. Once in place, failing well can become a team strength.

4. Learn fast. Admitting mistakes and building psychological safety into the team will make the team a secure place for review and input. This principle is often the starting point for teams. Making teams safe is a challenge for many and yet with safety comes the willingness for team members to speak up. In a fast changing environment, everyone's voice needs to be heard. So noticing when team members are dismissed rather than valued, are ridiculed rather than appreciated, is the first step towards safety. Creating space where team members are given the opportunity to explain their idea to an attentive audience is a powerful next step.

Exercise 12: Change readiness checklist

Effective leaders maintain an open mindset and are always on the lookout for new ideas, innovations, or new ways of doing things. They have found a powerful balance between maintaining their unique leader identity and also adapting it to the changing needs of their environment. Consider these questions:

1. What is your typical reaction to change (this may be personal or professional)? Do you dread it or embrace it?

2. If you look back over the past few months, have there been instances when certain aspects of your leadership approach have been embraced by others? What were you doing?

3. When you consider your working environment, which aspects of your leadership approach have been less successful and may need to be adapted or updated?

4. Are you reluctant to do this? If so, what is getting in your way?

Adopting an inclusive mindset

The highest result of education is tolerance. – Helen Keller

Inclusivity in your leadership approach means valuing and embracing 'difference' in the people around you, including people of a different age, gender, culture, race, and background. This mindset is fundamental to great leadership as we move into an era of higher complexity and global connectedness with people from different cultures and generations working together. This outlook is not as common as you may think and in many workplaces it is a powerful perspective that is ignored or resisted.

A good way to understand the core of an inclusive mindset is to consider the following questions:

1. Which aspects of leadership are valued in your workplace? For example, is competition highly valued? Or is

consultation and collaboration rewarded? One team session where a courageous member asked this exact question stands out for me. He was unsure of the purpose of the team and wanted to know whether it was an information-sharing forum or one where collaborative decisions could be made. What he was really asking was whether the leadership here was directive or collaborative. The interesting aspect in this example is that his question revealed that every member had a different perspective. So, this team's work became about really understanding what leadership they were all contributing to as a group.

2. Which dominant leadership norms are prevalent? For example, are financial achievements lauded as celebrations of leadership?

3. Are there parts of yourself that you may be suppressing as a leader?

Gender awareness is one aspect of the broader diversity in our world and it represents a fundamental difference that every one of us falls into. We are each either male or female. However, recognition of gender as one aspect of inclusion still has a long way to progress. In fact, most leadership assessments did not include women in their research samples until as late as the 1990s! A recent client conversation highlights how much of the journey remains when it comes to adopting an inclusive outlook. This senior director justified his all-white, all-male team by pointing out that his business was based on merit, not on promoting people based on their gender or culture. He went on to state that he would be appalled if anyone was promoted for any other reason. Poignantly, this director was also head of a division highly skewed towards men at the senior level, yet with a balance of genders in middle management. If a culture of merit had actually been in place, then the natural law of evolution would have ensured a better balance of gender and ethnicity in his team. Yet he was not open to considering this perspective.

There is a vast body of literature in gender studies and leadership that points to the dominance of male definitions of leading. In many Western cultures, leadership is still defined in masculine terms such as competitiveness, assertiveness, and self-promotion. The imbalanced organisational demographics that exist for women at senior levels is a powerful indicator of gender dynamics in the workplace. Your level of awareness of gender dynamics in your workplace means your insight into the ways in which women and men are treated and whether they have the same opportunities and access to opportunities or resources. Being active and aware of the gender dynamics in your environment and in yourself is critical to changing them.

My research suggested that promoting critical insight into the gender aspects of organisational contexts – how gender is reproduced through organisational practices – is a learning opportunity for both women and men. Theories such as Heilman's 'lack of fit' (1983) and Eagly and Karau's 'role congruity' (2002) describe the ways in which leadership is defined in these male terms. The theories highlight that male-defined leadership expectations are misaligned for women (based on stereotypically female traits of community and nurturing). These theories propose that men's social roles (that is, the culturally shared set of beliefs about how men should behave) correspond with the domain of leadership whereas women's social roles do not. According to both theories, this misalignment leads to the prejudice women can face in accessing leadership roles, as well as negative evaluations of their performance.

A leader identity perspective takes this a step further by asking you to consider whether these male definitions are part of the model of leadership that you have internalised. From this perspective it becomes crucial to understand whether your own internal expectations of leadership are based on male norms. If so, these may be the first barrier to forming or strengthening your unique leader identity.

The work of our leader identity approach is to notice your internal mental models of leadership and to consider whether it is these gender expectations of leadership that may be holding you back from identifying as a leader. The real question is that if leadership was defined in more neutral terms or more overtly feminine *and* masculine terms, would this impact how you see yourself? One client had an epiphany when faced with filling the shoes of his predecessor. He was worried that his collaborative leadership identity would not resonate with his executive team, who were used to the assertive, dominant stance of their previous CEO. However, in reflecting on the conditioning that he and his peers had received, he realised that his own approach was just as valid and acceptable as any other interpretation of leading.

The second step in this conditioning is to ask yourself whether you need to let go of the ways in which you have been defining leadership. Is it time to create your own leadership model from a conscious place that celebrates all the uniqueness that you bring – regardless of whether you happen to be male or female? This inclusive definition of leadership is important for both men and women. In fact, there are many men who also feel excluded and alienated from the dominant masculine norms of leadership in their organisation. They will be the first to tell you that they don't attend Friday evening drinks and prefer to spend time with their children rather than attend a football game with their peers. This is a hugely important point when we consider that the gender norms for leadership don't work for either gender.

It is important to remember that this gender conditioning has in all likelihood happened unconsciously. It is not something that our world has stated openly but rather reflects the unstated norms that are still rife in many organisations. Another client's experience remains etched on my mind. She was sitting in a leadership training session with her peers and was on an all-male team, with a male manager. The session was aimed at motivating the team to persevere, perform better, and lead well. To help them do this, they were each given a copy of Sun Tzu's *The Art of War*. As she tells it, she remembers looking at the title of the book and being completely bewildered as to why it was being handed out – particularly if they were talking about leadership. At the time she didn't have the confidence to articulate her confusion, but rather watched on like a spectator as her male colleagues shared their leadership war stories. She says she remembers sitting there and honestly wondering what the connection was. As you can see, this was her first real experience of the hidden gender dynamics embedded in her workplace at the time. She couldn't 'see' the male definitions of leadership or the fact that her male peers were connecting over their common view that leadership was about winning, competition, and beating the other party. This was because this perspective was so far removed from her leader identity which focused on winning *together*. Her perspective still meant she had high expectations for performance but crucially, the 'killer instinct' that her male peers were discussing was completely foreign and not part of her leadership repertoire. In my travels, this type of experience has been recounted by many individuals from different backgrounds and cultures who have struggled with this outdated, male-defined notion of leading.

Having insight into gender also indicates the likelihood that you are aware of biases that can exist towards other diverse characteristics, including (but not limited to) age, culture, and ethnicity. Ethnically diverse workforces are on the increase as are a wider age range of workers. Tapping into the potential of these individuals requires you to think more inclusively about their needs. It requires you to be more curious and respectful and to value the differences you see. One client enjoys a hugely diverse range of employees in their front line. Yet they were quick to recognise that even though the teams were from so many different cultural backgrounds, they were only rewarding the one style of leadership. So, in reality, they had diversity without inclusion. Their work became about better understanding the default leader expectations that prevailed in their promotion and recognition systems and updating these with broader interpretations of leading and being successful in their organisation.

Specifically, an inclusive mindset asks us to suspend judgement on leaders from diverse backgrounds and instead look for the richness that this leadership diversity can generate. Rather than deriding difference, your opportunity lies in listening to the voices of leadership from different backgrounds, different life experiences, and learning from each of them. One client's leadership provides a great example of this practice at work. He managed an ethnically diverse team and was concerned that the communication within the team was not as effective as it could be. In checking in with each of his team members, he learnt that the Australian culture of mateship and peer-to-peer joking did not sit well with everyone. Indeed some team members, from different cultural backgrounds, not only didn't understand the jokes but felt alienated as a result. Out of this straightforward exercise, the team gained perspective on their habits and agreed to adjust their communication so that everyone was engaged. Not surprisingly this team is now a high performer within that business. This example is relevant because it gets to the heart of inclusion. Every time you engage in dialogue that questions a person's claim to leadership or excludes them, you undermine their sense of who they are as leaders and the opportunity to create a more accessible leadership paradigm for everyone.

Adopting an inclusive mindset involves challenging assumptions that leadership is a predominantly male domain where men lead and women follow. It is about creating dialogue that includes the incredible diversity that women leaders, older leaders, or diverse cultural leaders bring and it is a critical requirement for today. Our workplaces are more diverse in so many ways than ever before and whilst this diversity will continue to grow, your ability to embrace it will help underpin your success. I hope by now you are starting to rethink who you are as a leader and recognising that outdated norms in leadership are unhelpful to your success and the success of the people around you.

Exercise 13: Organisational inclusion questions

Gaining insight into the hidden norms is a gradual process and requires a level of critical insight into these unspoken dynamics. Asking questions of your organisation, like those listed below, can help you to ascertain the level of inclusiveness in your organisation. These are often hard to detect but can have a strong impact on the long-term careers of everyone. Sample questions include:

- Are your senior teams gender balanced?

- What difference in background (ethnicity/age/gender) do your teams represent?

- What is the gender representation of men and women at senior levels?

- Are men and women paid equally for equal work?

- Which leadership behaviours are rewarded?

- Who around you models an inclusive approach?

Building a more inclusive workplace is one of the hardest challenges organisations face today due to the ongoing prevalence of stereotypes, unconscious bias, and assumptions that every one of us have been conditioned with. Research supports the fact that individuals who are inclusive of gender tend to be inclusive of all other differences as well. In other words, once you recognise the power of being curious about everyone around you, you create an environment that taps into their potential. If you choose to be more inclusive of difference in the circles of influence that you operate, this can have a powerful impact on the culture at large.

Exercise 14: Self-inclusiveness questions

1. How high is your level of inclusion? (Please avoid assuming that you and those around you already act fairly in all situations. There is 50 years of research to support the fact that we make decisions about people that are different to us all the time and these decisions are not necessarily accurate or fair.)

2. Is inclusion something you do naturally or is it something you are consciously working on by being more curious of others?

3. How diverse is your team or organisation? If there is diversity, can you say that there is inclusion as well? (Remember, we can have high levels of diversity with people from all walks of life and still have an organisational culture that only values one group.)

4. Which daily actions can you take to be more inclusive?

5. Are there pockets of people in your workplace that are inclusive? If so, how can you leverage their approach across the business?

6. Is there someone who could benefit from your perspective on how to be more inclusive? Which useful tips or strategies could you suggest to them? This can be a highly personal topic so having the courage to help another with insight into this area can be hugely positive if managed well.

And finally, be mindful of your own biases. These are so ingrained that we have to be vigilant. Apply critical thinking to your decisions and actively seek out those that are different.

Chapter 7

External strategies to strengthen your leader identity

My research highlighted that there are two key enabling strategies that are *external* to you and which will you assist you in building your leader identity. These are: **Building your social resources and Validating others.**

Building your social resources

The term 'social resources' refers to role models, sponsors, mentors, peers, friends, executive coaches, and any other sources that you may have that support you in your career. The bottom line is that in order to thrive, you need to be connected. Success does not happen in isolation – it happens in connection with others. No matter what stage of your career you are in, your ability to create mutually beneficial relationships with them will set you apart. It is not enough to keep your head down and get the job done. It is not enough to think only of the needs of your team and not of your organisation. It is not enough to be siloed in your thinking and your approach. Cross-functional, cross-boundaries, more expansive thinking and better relationships are now fundamental requirements.

Importantly, with 'social resources' I am not referring to the one mentor who you may have in your life right now. Building your social resources refers to the fact that high performers have a kaleidoscope of support. Their support is both internal and external to their organisation and they are intentional about building these multiple relationships which they rely on for feedback, growth, and support. This interdependence is highlighted in Figure 7.1.

Figure 7.1: Building connections and social resources

The range, availability, and suitability of your social resources is a determining factor in strengthening your leader identity. One key reason for this is outlined in research by Professor Jane Dutton, at the University of Michigan's Ross School of Business, who found that the more social support that is available to individuals, the more likely they will endure difficult situations or take on greater challenges. Indeed, these high quality relationships underpin growth in your capability. If we map this back to the prevalence of change that is upon us, then having people around you to support you, to validate your choices, and to strengthen your leader identity becomes of prime importance.

Research by Dobrow and Higgins (2005) also demonstrated the importance of having a range and diversity of support – specifically role models – to career success. This research showed that a variety of role models was associated with increased career-related cognitive flexibility – that is, being able to handle the complexity of roles and the choices that need to be made. This is in keeping with wider research that suggested a variety of role models provided a greater opportunity for individuals to engage in adaptation strategies that contributed to their positive leader identity formation.

In my research, the ability of participants to learn from a variety of role models and adapt their repertoire of skills was a key enabler for their leader identity. One participant reflected, "I've had several people I've learned from along the way that I look up to and respect in all different facets, and these added to my leadership." What is important in this comment is that this participant recognised and was open to adapting her leadership approach based on what she witnessed. This is a subtle but important insight. Many individuals will tell you whom they admire as a role model in their network. However, the pool gets smaller when they can also admit that they give themselves *permission* to adapt some of these behaviours as their own. One client mentioned that he was totally upfront and comfortable with taking on aspects of two key managers in his career. He explained that one of his managers was well known for his passion in developing and advocating for the success of his team members. The other manager was known for his autonomy, treating his team as owners of their own business, and providing opportunities for them to grow. This client went on to explain that he has consciously added both of these attributes to his own leader identity. In this way, having vicarious access to others in leadership roles and opportunities for you to witness the success strategies of them can be an enabler to your own identity. Exposure to these individuals can provide you with very powerful examples of what to do and sometimes what not to do when it comes to leading.

My research highlighted that the strategies you use with these resources are vitally important to your development. This includes whether you imitate aspects of the leadership you like or adapt your behaviours based on what has been positively role-modelled for you. Interestingly, there are potential gender differences in the way leaders use their resources that need to be noted here as well. Ibarra and Petriglieri (2007) identified gender differences in the strategies employed with role models in the professional identity formation of lawyers transitioning to partner roles. Their research, conducted in a male-dominated law firm, demonstrated that women lawyers tended to use 'true-to-self' strategies (defined as relying on their own personal style and staying faithful to this in their roles). These strategies were different to the imitation and acquisitive strategies (defined as imitating and practising the behaviours of perceived successful role models) that were used by the male lawyers. The study found that the women's true-to-self strategies, when dealing with a potential role model, hindered their ability to achieve success in their partner role by limiting their capacity to adapt to or try on new behaviours. This is important when we remember that both achieving authenticity and openness to change are strategies to strengthen your leader identity. This finding gets to the heart of one of the key messages of this guide, which is that whilst it is important to achieve authenticity as a leader, it is just as important to remain open to adapting your behaviours as the circumstances arise.

The importance of how you work with your social resources is reinforced further in research by Donald Gibson (2004). His research found that females do use acquisitive strategies – for example imitation – with role models of both genders, but only when they are in environments that are demographically balanced. However, the research found that the women were less likely to do so in male-oriented organisations. What does this tell us about the many women working in these imbalanced cultures; or more importantly, the assistance they might need? Fundamentally, if you are a female reading this, your ability to adapt and actively try on different behaviours with your social resources – whilst remaining authentic to who you are – is important, regardless of whether you work in a gender-balanced or gender-imbalanced organisation. If you are not intentional about the ways in which you rely on and learn from your social resources, you may inadvertently miss vital new development opportunities.

Strengthening your leader identity means being open to change and allowing yourself to imitate the leadership behaviours of others. At the same time it also means finding the important balance where you can ensure that your authentic self shines through. Building your social resources means paying attention to what successful leaders are doing in your network, watching them, and actively trying their approaches for yourself. Some leaders are wonderful at diffusing tension by well-placed humour in meetings. Others are amazing at injecting the human element into strategy discussions or maintaining their humility in the face of great results. These are just some examples that highlight how learning from those around you is at the core of your developmental growth. Openness to other's leadership behaviours and skills can widen your own leadership repertoire and, in doing so, strengthen your leader identity.

Strategies to build your social resources

There are some simple strategies that can help you build your social resources and strengthen your identity. These come from first looking at your connections and deciding whether you are satisfied that your support network is strong. It is important to remember that often it is not the quantity of your connections but rather the quality of these relationships that really matter.

Many clients decide that strengthening their existing relationships is the best way forward. In doing this, they review how regularly they are in contact with their key supports, and identify people whose leadership approach they admire. They are also active in connecting with people outside of their organisation.

For example, reconnecting with previous managers or colleagues from other roles can be a powerful way to build connections. Diarising a regular coffee catch-up with a contact is a simple way to embed these connecting behaviours into your leadership repertoire. This is an important skill that improves with practice.

Becoming more active in professional and educational forums is another strategy. No matter your chosen path, there are always professional bodies or networking groups that are relevant if you are prepared to go looking. This is often an effective way to get access to a range of new contacts outside of your existing connections.

Strategies to help you build or strengthen your support also include:

- Grabbing your own mentor

- Working with a coach

- Joining a professional development circle

Grabbing your own mentor

Building your social support is a key enabler for your leader identity. Having a range of mentors, both informally and formally, inside and outside of your workplace, is a key development strategy. If you have not had the opportunity to work with a mentor, they are often in your network already.

Mentoring is traditionally recognised as a knowledge transfer from those more experienced to those less experienced, and tends to be area specific (for example, mentoring can be focused on strategy, workplace skills, interpersonal relationships to name a few.). Mentoring can offer new knowledge and perspectives that may be useful to the other person. Good mentoring practice is seen more as a collaborative learning alliance.

Predominantly, the key to successful mentoring is the degree to which it educates and empowers the person being mentored; however, there is considerable research to support the fact that mentors also benefit from the mentoring relationship. Mentors have the opportunity to fine-tune their own skills, communication, and leadership capabilities. Mentoring also provides a forum for mentors to decompress from their hectic days and focus their attention on helping others. This, in turn, has been shown to decrease stress levels and increase a sense of energy and rejuvenation.

Informal mentoring in organisations is a fantastic way for you to widen your scope and build your experience, education, and awareness of the business around you. These relationships are a great way to share ideas with someone who has the experience and can assist you to develop yourself and your career. In fact, the majority of mentoring happens informally. If you take the time to reflect on your day at work, there are natural mentors whom you frequently come in contact with. Interestingly, most business leaders feel that they are mentoring on a regular basis. Even if the advice is not given a formal title, many may be spending time with you, helping you to develop. If this is the case, then recognising this input and actively reflecting on it may be a simple way to enhance your resources.

In mentoring, every conversation is a possible learning opportunity. Your ability to listen and be present with your mentor will actually improve the quality of the relationship. In listening attentively, research shows that you improve the other person's ability to think. In essence, a good mentoring relationship is when the two of you establish that you are in fact equal thinking partners. They may have more expertise in a certain area, hence the reason you are meeting, but this doesn't stop you from asking insightful questions that help them with their own reflections and development. Remember the underlying premise that every individual is in a constant process of forming or reforming their leader identity. So, do not defer to their experience in a way that undermines your ability to show up confidently. Rather ensure your attention is in the moment and you are prepared to ask questions that contribute to the mutual learning for the two of you.

If you want to engage in a mentoring relationship, there are some fundamental areas you need to consider:

- What is it that you want to achieve from the mentoring? What is the core purpose? You will need to be able to clearly articulate this to your proposed mentor. A simple classification is: Are you looking for professional career guidance, or are you looking for more relationship support?

- How will you select your mentor? It is useful here to consider what values and ethics you see the people around you displaying, as this often forms the core premise of good vs bad mentoring experiences. Ask yourself, who in the business or in your life in general has the depth of experience that you would like to tap into?

- What preparation do you need to do to ensure your mentoring meetings are worthwhile? Here I recommend that you come to the meetings with clear areas you would like to discuss and some insightful questions that will assist with your message.

- What degree of confidentiality would you propose for the meetings? This is a fundamental area for success or failure as both parties must discuss and agree to the confidentiality parameters. For example, will you be happy with your mentor discussing your goals with their peers? Or would you prefer that your discussions remain 100% confidential between the two of you? Also, how much will you disclose to your colleagues? Will you both let people within the organisation know that you have a mentoring relationship?

- How will you know when the mentoring has worked? Which goals will you set and how will you monitor them?

One thing we do know now about mentoring is that it is only successful when the interpersonal relationship is strong. By interpersonally strong, I mean that there is confidence in your relationship and trust that it will go well. This can only emerge by being clear about your expectations for each other and by actively using these expectations in your meetings. In your first meeting with your mentor, as well as following the five steps, there is an opportunity to tell them who you are and what leadership means to you. In being courageous in opening the dialogue this way, you have the opportunity to shortcut the usual conversation and get straight into the dialogue that will make a difference, potentially to you both.

Building your social resources means connecting with others in ways that build mutually beneficial relationships that will sustain you over your career. I mentioned the WIN conference in Prague earlier and I mention it again here for its wise approach in helping people connect with one another with purpose and with pleasure. Kristen Envig, the founder, handed out simple connecting cards with the following advice: "Be open and ready to connect, be quick to contribute, take a risk, commit, and be prepared to experience magic."

Working with a coach

Coaching has experienced tremendous growth in the past 15 years where three types of development needs are typically addressed. These needs are skills acquisition, performance enhancement, and leadership development. Research by Brian Underhill and his team in 2014 highlighted that 97% of organisations surveyed utilise coaching services for leader development. This is in part driven by the need to tailor development to the individual needs of clients, particularly as they engage in more complex roles. In keeping with the shift toward more collaborative leadership and supporting leaders at every level, there has also been a growth in internal coaching services within organisations, as well as managers coaching their teams.

Research has supported the positive role that engaging with a coach can have in building your social support and accessing a wider repertoire of behaviours. Coaching is a collaborative learning process designed to help you achieve your goals and expand your thinking abilities. Perhaps more importantly, an effective coaching relationship is one where you as the client can explore and challenge your own perspectives in a constructive, forward-looking environment. A skilled coach is able to help you identify the strategies you are currently employing and can mirror back to you opportunities for change or growth.

Given my own background in executive coaching, I am particularly supportive of coaching in the leader development arena. Whilst there is huge value in building your leader identity through group training and workshops, it is often through the personalised reflection in coaching that real change is achieved.

However, finding a coach who is capable of supporting your needs requires your attention. Most countries now have coaching organisations, such as the International Coaching Federation (ICF), as well as a range of tertiary institutions offering university qualifications in coaching. It is important to note that there are no professional standards or barriers to entry in coaching. However, there is great activity going on to develop the robustness of coaching with initiatives such as the Institute of Coaching's mandate to build the evidence base of coaching worldwide. In my view, a university qualification is a worthwhile minimum filter when selecting a coach. However, it must be said that whilst coach training can be a safety net, it is not a guarantee that the coach is suitable or capable of meeting your needs.

Finding a coach who can support your leader development means talking to your network and finding those who have worked with people you know or know of. Similarly, approaching coaching organisations in your area or asking your HR team for references is also worthwhile. Meeting with more than one coach will give you the opportunity to clarify whose approach will best suit you. Being prepared for these meetings with your list of incisive questions will send a very clear message to a prospective coach that you are serious about your development.

From a leader identity perspective, it is also helpful to query a prospective coach on their views on leadership. Asking about their worldviews on hierarchy and collaboration or using the stakeholder interview questions in Chapter 5 will help uncover some of their biases and beliefs. It may also be worth knowing which leadership models they support and which development tools they use. All of this will help you to appreciate in greater detail whether their approach is one that will constructively challenge your own.

Finally, when it comes to coaching to develop your leader identity and build your support, there is also a robust school of thought that a good coach will be open to go on a learning journey with you. This means that with all the tools and perspectives the coach can share, the real ability is for you both to co-create you leader development path towards one that is full of possibility. The idea that you can lead regardless of your age, your experience, or your background is one that is open to your interpretation. Your coach may partner with you to make this a reality in ways you cannot yet envisage.

Joining a professional development circle

Finding a community that shares your values and supports your goals is getting easier with the rise in leader circles or various goal circles, chapters, and network groups around the world. These communities are arising due to the demand for forums where individuals can connect and tap into informal networks for career, business, or personal support. The success of these groups is based on the fact that members are there for mutual assistance, to listen, to understand, and to ensure that every voice is heard. This peer-to-peer learning environment is a wonderful way to test out your leader identity and to build your support network and connections.

Tips to strengthen your social resources

- If you are keen to develop your social support, it is often more effective to spend 80% of your time on strengthening your existing connections and 20% on establishing new relationships. This is particularly true if you have a fairly established network.

- Best practice means building the quality of your relationships, not necessarily the quantity. This can be fairly time effective and can often be done 1 hour a week or 15 minutes a day. Consistency is the key to getting results here.

- Consider integrating your connections into your daily activities. Projects, committees, and group assignments provide a great opportunity to set the stage for further discussions.

- Social media is a no-brainer – particularly with the ease of LinkedIn in connecting with others.

- It is fine to have 'transactional' style connections; just ensure you 'cut to the chase' and ask for what's needed. Asking for what you need is a wonderful strength.

- Ask yourself whether you could be a sponsor or mentor. Consider reciprocity; what have you given others before they have asked?

- Consider a relationship action plan for your top 10 contacts that will keep them firmly on your radar. Even a yearly catch-up can be enough to keep the relationship strong if this expectation is agreed between the two of you.

Great leaders are incredibly proactive and intentional about building relationships with people over their careers. They recognise the power of sustaining long-term relationships and of regularly communicating with their connections. For many, this is not on a 'to-do' list, but rather embedded in their way of working.

Exercise 15: Social resource reflections

1. How proactive are you in building relationships related to your career? Remember, this can be people with whom you work, study, or socialise.

2. What are you doing in service of your connections? Remember, any connection is a reciprocal relationship and it is far more powerful to consider what you can give than what you can receive.

3. How important is it to you to expand your connections? What ideas do you have for this?

4. How important is it to you to strengthen your existing connections? What activities could support you in this?

Validating others

Who am I being that their eyes aren't shining? – Benjamin Zander

Validating others is at the core of a culture of collaboration. This strengthening strategy refers to your recognition and actions in confirming, supporting, and encouraging the leadership qualities in the people around you. Being willing and able to notice the strengths, values, talents, and capabilities in people helps them to become what they are capable of being. This social validation may come from peers, managers, and external others, and it helps every individual internalise a leader identity as a part of who they are. This is important for two reasons:

Firstly, this approach contributes to a more empowered, inclusive culture by acknowledging how leadership can be shared and is not reliant on positional power.

Secondly, in the spirit of reciprocity, every time you validate the leadership quality of someone else, you reinforce both their sense of who they are as leaders as well as your own. This mindset acknowledges that, in validating someone else, you are also validating a wonderful gift of your own – being prepared to be a leader who can share leadership with others.

Leadership is a social process. When we choose to lead, our leadership is either validated or undermined by the people around us. Every time we receive encouragement from our peers, manager, friends or family it helps us to internalise our leader identity as a part of our inner self. This helps makes sense of those powerful 'a-ha' moments that you have experienced where someone in your life may have changed the way you thought about yourself.

Many clients have reflected on their own journey, and like many of us, have reported their share of enablers and derailers. By enablers I mean experiences that have supported who they are as leaders and that have served them well in the evolution of their personal growth. On the flipside, many have also experienced difficult episodes and events that have 'derailed' and undermined their sense of themselves as leaders.

A positive example that I personally had very early in my career was about integrity and ethics in leadership. I was in my first management role, responsible for buying products for a national retailer. I had heard through the grapevine that one senior buyer was taking 'rewards' from suppliers for buying their products. I raised this knowledge with my manager at the time, who simply stated, "Suzi, remember that if you accept a bribe, make sure it lasts your entire lifetime." This was such a straightforward statement, yet it has stayed with me to this very day. Two very important things were reinforced for me in that moment: 1) my manager validated my independence and autonomy as a leader by inferring that it was up to me to decide, and 2) he reinforced my own internal value of ethics at work. This was a simple 'a-ha' moment that emphasised the fundamental premise of ethics in my career and which remains a cornerstone of my leader identity today.

Take a moment to think about a person in your life who has validated you as a leader – perhaps they saw a strength in you that you did not see? They may be a teacher, a friend, or a manager. What did they do? How did it change your thinking about yourself?

These micro moments are so important because every time the people around you accept your view, your input, and your direction, they are validating your influence, or in our language, your leader identity. This is not the same as demanding that your views must be agreed with or acted upon. Rather, this is about acknowledging when your views are taken into account and accepted by others. This social dynamic is critical in continuing to internalise your leader identity.

Leaders who do this well are active in creating a culture of shared leadership and finding ways to empower others to lead. They are open in recognising the leadership qualities of the people around them and practise creating opportunities to tap into their leadership potential – whether it is through creating projects to lead or activities to drive. This willingness to share and promote the leadership prospects of others is a foundational aspect of high-performing cultures and it is something to be celebrated.

Yet often we see the hierarchical mindset firmly in place. It can show up in dynamics such as not valuing the leadership of the younger generations. This is often tied to entrenched views which value years of experience over thinking ability. This trend reminds me of a session with 120 students. In a school environment where the hierarchical positions of leadership are very limited, these students embraced the concept of leadership as a way of being and shared their incredible stories of support and of taking responsibility. The stories ranged from one participant choosing to continue the legacy left by her late grandfather in distributing warm blankets to the homeless, to another student who made a point of bringing food to share with less fortunate friends. Here's what one of the participants had to say about her unique positive influence:

> "My father is in the military, therefore I have moved around a lot as a kid. Always going to different schools, I realised I am adaptable and flexible. I am always walking up to people asking if they would like a friend."

And from another:

> "When I was in the ninth grade, I suffered from depression. I have now recovered and believe I am of help to others who are suffering. I listen to other young people my age to help them know they are not alone."

However, as we have seen in earlier chapters, the appetite and readiness to recognise the leader potential in others is often not shared across organisations. This perspective may be one that you are finding hard to reconcile yourself. Certainly clients have disagreed with the premise that the qualities of leadership exist within every individual based on their personal experience of poor performers. One client became quite agitated as he outlined how he could not get his front-line staff to take responsibility for their actions, let alone to lead. This type of behaviour is not uncommon. How can the premise stand true if the actions do not support it?

This is not an easy dilemma to solve. The employee disengagement statistics quoted earlier give credence to the fact that many employees are far from delivering their best or, in our language, staying true to their leader identity. However, we need to find ways to break this cycle. Adopting different perspectives to a common challenge is a powerful way to do this. A leader identity perspective requires you to think differently and to ask different questions. In the example of the agitated client earlier, we went down this question path together:

- What are you missing out on if you don't acknowledge that every individual has the *potential* to lead?

- How would your approach be different if you opened yourself to the possibility that the qualities of leadership exist within everyone?

- What would be different for your teams if they were treated as leaders or potential leaders?

- What processes or procedures could be changed to empower them to take more responsibility?

- How can you identify new and creative ways for leadership to be shared?

These questions are not the solution to the challenge; however, they are guaranteed to open up a different dialogue. As we know, different dialogue leads to different solutions and who knows what hidden strength or talent lies underneath?

Asking managers and those in positions of power to reality-check their assumptions is a powerful starting point. The conditioning of the hierarchy is all pervasive and being able to notice this conditioning and to challenge it is a powerful, empowering mindset. This was brought home by the insight that one senior leader had when considering the degree to which he validated others. He was honest in his response that, up until our session, he had only validated the leadership potential of others when they showed leadership qualities that were similar to his own! In fact, he realised that he had been quite dismissive or blind to the qualities of others outside his own definition of what leadership looked like. As you can imagine, this was a light-bulb moment for him. In that moment he recognised that the way he was being as a leader was potentially suppressing the leadership qualities of those around him. Instead, he began to see that if he were to ask different questions, to be different as a leader, then different behaviours would result. Perhaps he would start to see that the qualities of leadership exist within everyone; however, this is only feasible if he was willing to acknowledge this possibility.

If you are uncertain about the potential in validating the leadership potential in others, I invite you to check out the HBR/McKinsey Leaders Everywhere Challenge of 2013 mentioned earlier. There are a number of case studies on this website that point to the appetite of individuals to lead. This is particularly true of those individuals within organisations who removed some of the hierarchical restrictions and were pleasantly surprised at the willingness of individuals to step up and into their leadership potential. Validating others is a mindset that will assist you to tap into this latent potential and unlock the leadership capability of the people around you – one person at a time.

Finally, validating others can be as simple as genuinely connecting with others, giving authentic feedback, and providing small recognitions of gratitude. Being consistent in these behaviours will enable a true culture of collaboration.

You cannot underestimate the relevance of helping others to lead in building your own leader identity. Every time you acknowledge or support the leadership efforts of another, you are in effect supporting your own. You become known as the leader who is unafraid to recognise effort when it is due, and you do this because you understand that in validating them, you are providing them with wonderful recognition. You are also validating yourself.

Exercise 16: Questions to validate others

Here are some more thought starters that may come in handy:

- How can you more actively validate the leadership potential of others?

- Which activities have been particularly useful in empowering others to lead?

- How can you share this perspective with others who may not be comfortable with this mindset?

- What would you need to be more curious about in order to tap into the potential of others?

- How often do you ask your colleagues what they need to realise their leadership potential?

- How often do you put yourself in the shoes of the people with whom you are communicating, and consider whether you are providing them with opportunities to lead?

- How regularly do you acknowledge their values and goals and assist them in achieving them? (Remember, most of us like to be heard and acknowledged – even if you don't feel you are in a position to make a difference to their goals, your presence and attention will.)

- How do you create an environment where those around you are not afraid to share their thoughts or feelings and speak up?

- Do you know how those around you like to be recognised? How would you rate your positivity actions (i.e. the positivity ratio of 3 – 1)?

Exercise 17: Strategies to enable your leader identity

Now it is time to reflect on all of the themes that may strengthen your leader identity covered in these two chapters.

Fill in the ideas that are relevant to you in the following table:

My potential enablers	Impact/10 _Degree to which they are strengthening my leadership self, where 0=no impact; 10=high impact_	Actions I will take to strengthen these (or add these into my plans)
External enablers: • • • • • • •		
Self-enablers: • • • • • • •		

If you haven't been able to capture all of the areas covered in these chapters, fill in some additional ideas in the following table:

Strategies	Actions I will take
My definition of leadership	
Achieving authenticity	
Being change-ready	
Adopting an inclusive mindset	
Building social resources	
Validating others	

Chapter 8

Protecting your leader identity

Never let a good crisis go to waste. – Winston Churchill

With all the positivity of the preceding chapters, it would be remiss not to address the reality of trying to lead and the difficulties one can face in such an intention. In fact, your leader identity runs the risk of being undermined or derailed every day. As such, this chapter is focused on the elements that can derail you in your leadership. I use the word 'derail' as it is particularly relevant to the experiences of research participants, clients, and colleagues. A definition of derail is: *To cause to be deflected from a purpose or direction, permanently or temporarily; to go astray* (Random House Dictionary, 2014). Research by D. Scott DeRue and colleagues (2009) showed that where your leader identity is not validated by others – such as encountering various career obstacles – this may call into question this aspect of who you are.

My research highlighted that wherever you work, it is important to recognise there are many obstacles that can destabilise your leader identity or even halt your leader formation process. One client recently highlighted that she did not feel confident speaking up in meetings in a way that reflected who she really was.

She felt there were unspoken rules in her leadership team which meant she was afraid to really bring all of herself to the table. Like many teams, this meant the real decision making and authentic discussion happened outside of the meeting. However, as you can imagine, this lack of authenticity was having a very real impact on her motivation levels. This is not uncommon. Experiencing derailers can lead to disengagement and even opting out of the role altogether. Like in this client's situation, derailers are often hidden and very hard to detect.

Consider your own life experiences. Has something happened to you, or was initiated by you, that has deflected you from your life's purpose or your authentic self? Have you experienced a time in your life where you have been on the wrong path? Have you taken on feedback that has stopped your career development? I will never forget one colleague who was told by a recruitment firm that he had failed their IQ test and was not smart enough to be considered. Can you imagine what this feedback did to his sense of self? And what on earth was he meant to do with this information? The only thing that soothes this memory is the fact that two months later he was recruited by a global firm to head their treasury function and has not looked back. These are just a few of the ways in which can be derailed from our path – and most importantly from our potential to lead.

Like the internal and external enabling strategies, my research highlighted that derailers tend to be factors that are external to us (like the stormy weather in Figure 8.1, over page) and those that are internal to us (things that can undermine our inner selves – or in the case of the tree metaphor, damage our roots).

Another client's experience highlights these internal and external derailers well. He had been in a management role for a multinational telecommunications firm for six months and had accepted the position for the international experience it would provide. Within months of being in the new organisation, he was offered a position in their international head office. Metaphorically, as soon as the offer was verbally made, his bags were packed!

However, two weeks later he hadn't received confirmation of the international role from his local manager. A week later he arrived at the global head office for another meeting, and was informed that his local manager had blocked his promotion. He was given the rationale that the offer was withdrawn as the company couldn't proceed with the role without the agreement of the local office, to avoid accusations of poaching. As he tells it, the news felt like a physical body blow. As well as impacting his future career, the blocking by his local manager went against every belief he held about leadership, particularly his own passion in developing those around him.

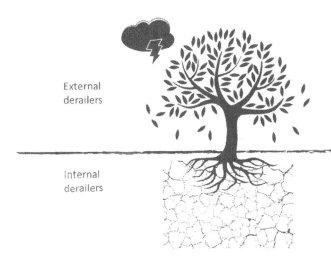

External
derailers

Internal
derailers

Figure 8.1: Metaphor for internal and external derailers

On his return, he worked up the courage to raise the issue with his local manager and was met with flat denial. He knew first-hand that his local manager was responsible for the decision. However, in the retelling of this experience, he also realised that he had not cultivated the relationships in the organisation to gain support in influencing a different outcome. Eventually, without the acknowledgement of his manager, this client ended up unconsciously internalising the withdrawal of the offer as something that he was responsible for. From a leader identity perspective, the external derailer (a blocked promotion by his manager) also acted as an internal derailer which undermined his confidence and leader identity. It took him a little while to regain his equilibrium and not long after, he was making plans to exit the organisation.

This client regrets how he handled the adversity and the amount of time it took for his confidence to return. His regret is centred mainly on the fact that he did not seek support to help navigate the politics. He also regretted not having the courage to hold his local manager accountable so that he could prevent him from stymying someone else's career. However, through his development, he has conceded that the experience was one of the most formative for his own leadership – highlighting all the behaviours he never wanted to adopt. Today he remains an enabling leader and has plenty of stories of where team members have benefitted from his generous mentoring and advocacy in their career progression.

I tell this story because these are so many potential derailers, obstacles, and challenges that can undermine the formation of your leader identity. This is because, as we have seen, leadership is not only a personal process (based on your unique personal traits, characteristics, and history) but a social process too; highlighting the importance of both organisational and social contexts.

External derailers

My research highlighted that external derailers fall into three key categories: navigating organisational cultures, life/home decisions, and embedded institutional mindsets. It is important to remember that you may not have faced any of these, or you may be familiar with all of them. The point is that the pathway to leadership is different for everyone, and therefore your ability to notice them and navigate these challenges is paramount.

Derailer 1: Navigating organisational cultures

In corporate life, there are many subtle ways that organisational context can negatively influence how individuals conduct themselves at work or how they can be derailed from who they really are. Organisational climate (which at worst can include negativity or gossip), culture (results at all costs), behavioural norms ('face time', inflexibility) and politics (low trust and sometimes a lack of confidence in leadership) can condition people in harmful ways. For many people working in these environments, this can bring about a self-censoring of their opinions or an unintended consequence of disengaging from their roles. A recent example of this came from a client who was considering a senior career move, but was hesitant to make the change due to his experience of working with difficult leaders. His lack of trust in the leaders in his company had been internalised as his own uncertainty of who he had become as a leader or who he may become. Had he not taken the time to reflect on these underlying dynamics, he was potentially going to turn down a pivotal career move based on unhelpful assumptions. Instead, he worked on his own leader identity and minimised his uncertainty by reconnecting to his unique talents, courage, and beliefs, which freed him to lead in his own way.

Navigating negative cultures is a very real challenge for many people. These cultures may arise as the result of relentless change or deficits such as the absence of good leadership. Negativity can arise in the everyday events of difficult conversations, in the power plays, and organisational politics – all of which can contribute to perceived unfairness and all-round toxicity. When I ask teams which organisational derailers they may be facing, it doesn't take long for them to identify them. However, these teams have very rarely connected the fact that these environmental derailers can undermine their own sense of self. They are not just a laundry list of complaints, but rather very real obstacles that can see people disengaging, becoming part of the problem, or in the worst case-scenario, opting out altogether.

As we have seen in this guide, the activities to mediate these common challenges involve each individual taking up the reins of leadership for themselves, to self-lead in a way which is validating and positive both for their own wellbeing and for their peers. In taking ownership of their own leader identity, they retain their ability to continue to contribute and make good judgements in the face of adversity. I would go so far as to say that in extreme circumstances, taking ownership of your leader identity is a survival mechanism.

Those of you who are familiar with gender norms will recognise that these are harmful for both men and women. According to the International Labour Organisation (ILO, 2009), gender norms represent the socially constructed expectations of men and women and their unique needs in terms of their individual roles, responsibilities, opportunities, and constraints in the workplace. For women, navigating organisational climates can entail all the reported obstacles of the so-called 'Glass Labyrinth', a term coined by researchers Eagly and Carli (2007). This metaphor symbolises the range and variety of hidden difficulties women can face when navigating their careers, which in many organisations can lead to the progressive decline in women at every stage. The literature suggests that a range of gender issues exist for women, including a lack of access to formal and informal networks (Piterman, 2008), along with a sense of psychological isolation and tokenism (Eagly and Karau, 2002). Other noted career barriers for women navigating organisational climates include difficulty in being promoted (Rhode and Kellerman, 2007), and the prevalence of sex-stereotyped roles, whereby leadership roles are typically seen in masculine, agentic terms and support roles in more communal, feminine terms (Eagly, 2005). Indeed, Eagly and Carli (2007) pointed out that a double bind of leadership behaviour exists due to gender stereotypes, showing that women may face negative reactions when they take charge and yet they may be considered a poor leader if they fulfil the gender stereotype of being kind. You may recall this concept underpinned a story I told earlier, regarding the minefield that women can face in trying to achieve authenticity as a leader. Finally, a lack of role models of women in leadership roles has also been cited as a key barrier.

However, difficulty navigating organisational climates is not solely the challenge for women. For men this can entail the challenges of living up to outdated norms about the alpha male leader and of having to compete for organisational definitions of success. Unfortunately, in many situations, data shows that the social and organisational context in which individuals aspire to leadership positions seem largely unsupportive if the individual challenges these organisational norms. There are many examples of men who have been covertly penalised by their workplace for not wanting to take the next step up in the hierarchy. This is often viewed as a reflection of their lack of commitment rather than their expression of who they are. In fact, men are more likely than women to be penalised in this regard. Many male clients have spoken about the limitations they feel in the expectations for them to continue to strive and continue to emulate the leader norms around them.

In terms of internalising unhelpful organisational norms, one client realised she was far too serious and assertive at work. Her team rarely saw her enjoying a good laugh and this was impacting on her workplace relationships. Through building her self-awareness, she came to see that she had unconsciously internalised the organisation's expectation for leadership as her own. She worked in a very serious, conservative firm and these characteristics had gradually and unwittingly been adopted as her own. And she was unhappy. Outside of work, her friends knew her as warm, caring, and fun; however, this aspect of her identity was not evident in her workplace. So she simply decided to give herself permission to bring her entire identity to work and to build enjoyment into her working week. This involved simple things like taking her team out for 'walking meetings', introducing shared-lunch Friday, and personally connecting with people over issues outside of work. It was these small changes that had a lasting impact. She was able to realise this aspect of her identity and relish living it.

Another potential derailer in organisational cultures is getting access to the right people and ensuring you are connected. As we have seen in the enablers, your success is driven in a large part by your ability to establish and deepen your people connections. Difficulty in accessing these networks can include being considered part of the 'new guard', when the culture values those with length of service. Or it can be seen in functional silos which value certain divisions and not others. Or it can show up in old boys' networks which can alienate both men and women who do not share the same educational background or history.

These outdated organisational norms and assumptions can derail any leader identity. These potential derailers exist for individuals in the workplace every day, and reinforce the notion that each person needs to remain mindful of who they are at work, or who they aspire to be. As in the last example, we shape and are shaped by our organisational cultures, so the concept of remaining vigilant about how you are showing up is key.

Finding potential solutions to these organisational derailers can be as straightforward as investigating the following three questions:

1. What stories are you or your team telling one another about these issues? Where are the common links?
   In answering these questions, you are likely to identify some of the core derailers.

2. Which forces impact the way things are working right now? How much alignment is there in the recognition of these?

In answering this question and identifying where there is a lot of alignment, you are likely to be able to prioritise the main issues.

3. What stories do you wish they would tell that would ameliorate this derailer?

In answering this question, you are able to start to create new solutions.

In the boys' club example, being able to showcase where people of different backgrounds have added value is a powerful way to break down outdated mentalities. This is just one example; however, I recommend you allow yourself plenty of scope to be creative – there are many solutions to a problem. Often we need to allow ourselves the freedom to find them.

It is also important to note that many organisational cultures are not negative and many companies have been actively updating their ways of working. These inclusive, strengths-based cultures are on the rise. Within them, individuals are valued for their uniqueness, and their individual sense of self is often rewarded and validated. The good news is that these environments are enjoying the fruits of their cultures. They recognise that every individual has a role to play in their collective future and they are on their way to empowering more people to have a positive influence.

Derailer 2: Life, family and home decisions

There is plenty of research on and recognition of the role of caring responsibilities, workload, and lack of balance in derailing one's career and leader identity challenges which apply to both men and women. We will cover each of these separately.

Caring responsibilities

According to research by McKinsey (2012), career attitudes among women and men are converging both in terms of the degree of ambition and aspirations. Despite this convergence, the barrier of the double burden of balancing home with the demands of work is highlighted by many individuals and is considered to be a potential derailer in maintaining their leadership role. These caring responsibilities are not just limited to having children; in fact, research shows that we will all be challenged with caring for elderly parents or relatives over our careers. Caring responsibilities will touch everyone's lives.

In my research, the perspective of a leader with four school-age children captured her challenge: "You can keep all the balls in the air and keep going and keep performing at work and you can keep a happy family. But suddenly it just all catches up on you. When you're in that stage, you have a real chance of derailing."

This classic derailer is reported on widely – particularly the impact of parenting on career growth. One example comes from a colleague who had approached his manager to access paid parental leave. His partner had just given birth to their first child and, serendipitously, the company had just announced paid parental leave for both carers. His male manager responded to his request to access the new parental leave policy with the following statement: "The answer is no and don't you ever ask me that question again." There it was – the penalty for trying as a male to take on caring responsibilities (the domain stereotypically belonging to females). He was appalled at this response and also to learn that this new policy was in reality only given lip-service by the business.

The impact of life decisions such as family and career breaks has been well researched by Hewlett and Luce (2005) and is particularly insightful. Their research looked at the impact of parental leave on the careers of women, which can often occur at a critical career juncture for many, with career growth and parenthood frequently clashing. Their term 'on-ramping' is relatively new and is gaining credence in organisations. 'Off-ramping' and 'on-ramping' refer to the avenues women and men can take in transitioning out of and back into work. Importantly, their research found that on-rampers were hungry for help, with 94% of the 5,000 women surveyed reporting they would like help transitioning back in. These women felt that a variety of company-sponsored initiatives would make for more successful reintegration.

Transitions such as returning from parental leave can have a lasting impact on your identity. An individual on-ramping back into work may want to test out a variety of different possibilities (hours, responsibilities, income, promotion, etc.) that fit with their new evolving sense of identity. This process may be straightforward for some, but for others this can be a very fraught time. Why? Because every individual at some point over their transition is weighing up the pros and cons of their different identities. Having just been in a situation where they are coming to terms with their identity as a parent, returning to work means reorienting their thinking towards their professional identities and their identity as a leader. My research has shown that even the most committed worker can find the transition back into work more trying than they expected. This is often because there is a longer psychological process involved. At an identity level, they are effectively making room in their heads for the new identity they are adopting – and also getting rid of some of the old identities that may still be in place. As one client reflected, "I feel like I am a totally different person to the one who walked out the office door six months ago. Now I am both a mother and a leader and it all feels very unsettled."

Thankfully, a growing number of companies have begun to recognise the relevance of these transitions and introduced support programs to help meet the challenge. My research showed that the parental leave journey is a particularly individual one and catering to the individual needs of each employee is critical to reintegrating employees in a sustainable way that will ensure their career longevity and success.

Workload

Not surprisingly, workload is another potential identity derailer. How can we expect individuals to lead authentically if they are burnt out or exhausted? The pervasive 24/7 mentality – the expectation of the ideal worker who is available at all times without any family responsibilities such as children or aging parents – lies at the heart of so many disengaged workers, and it is equally prevalent for men and women. Research by Erin Reid, associate professor in Organisational Behaviour at Boston University, highlighted that some men use under-the-radar coping strategies to maintain an image of the ideal worker and to avoid penalty. These men don't formalise their family priorities, but rather maintain their 24/7 illusion by pursuing strategies such as seeking local clients and thereby minimising their travel commitments. Her research also showed that the men and women who were upfront about their needs outside of their workplace were still marginalised. So, when it comes to workload and the all-illusive work-life balance, there is still plenty of work to be done. This organisational norm plays havoc with the wellbeing of many individuals. An article in the *New York Times* revealed that employees on Wall Street were 1.5 times more likely to commit suicide than the national average if they did not have regular time off.

In an effort to address this potential derailer, shifting one's attitude to think about needs in terms of integrating work and life is an important reframe. Work-life integration is about living your life as a whole, for the good of yourself and the people around you. Your work and your life exist as a unit; they are actually inseparable. You move across these different domains but the common denominator of them is you – your personality, skills, talent, and your unique characteristics. So, work-life integration is about finding ways in which these two domains can exist together in harmony so that you are motivated and inspired.

The definition of integration commonly means putting together, joining, and assimilating. The goal is to combine aspects of yourself in each domain, which allows you to feel more energised and nourished. A modern concept of managing work and life is to be able to devote the right amount of energy to the various areas of your life so that you will feel energised and rejuvenated. To illustrate this, I am reminded of a client who was at the point of despair with his work. He was ready for a change from the long hours and travel expectations, yet, from the organisation's perspective, his loss would have had major repercussions for the business. He was torn between his loyalty for the business and his need for something to restore his energy levels. His solution was not to resign and move on, but rather to integrate his way of working and living. Coaching identified that his love of challenges and adrenalin was missing from his life. So, in the time he had outside of work, he decided to pick up his love for racing cars (extreme, I know, but it worked for him). This hobby fulfilled his personal needs and actually resulted in him feeling more focused and satisfied at work, even though his work commitments remained steady. Whenever a presentation arose, he would use his latest racing experience to highlight his message, and his passion was evident for all to see. Through this integration, the quality of his work increased, as did the quality of his life.

Lack of boundaries

The challenge in balancing work and life is one that commonly derails one's best intentions. Taking the time to stop to actually reflect and really tune in to who you are being at work and who you aspire to be, is not common. And yet the benefits of stopping, taking stock, and reflecting are well founded. This simple action allows you to replenish your mental reserves and enhance your mental energy. Stopping allows you to reflect on your real priorities, align your feelings, thoughts, and behaviours, and give yourself the mental energy boost needed to ensure that your leader identity is being realised. My hope is that somewhere in this guide you are stopping to do the exercises and really think about who you are as a leader.

The concept of harnessing and developing your mental energy is a concept that has gained a great deal of momentum. Globally, those in the helping professions such as coaches, psychologists, and human resource professionals, are focused on the importance of mental energy as the basis for their clients' performance and wellbeing. This is because when we are feeling highly energised, our motivation and ability to perform are enhanced. When our energy levels are low, the opposite can be true.

These energy levels can shift on a daily basis. Work performance can vary from days of extreme productivity to days where even the smallest task feels like a huge challenge. It can also lead to days when your thinking is crystal clear and 'on the money', and others when it is just a lot harder to get it together and 'think straight'. We are affected by our mental energy levels on a daily basis – whether we are consciously aware of this influence or not.

By slowing down – whether it is a break of ten minutes or an hour – we are able to notice ourselves again. We are able to stop the busy thinking and just relax in our bodies. Obviously there are techniques that can help us do this even more effectively than just stopping. Relaxation techniques, engaging in creative pursuits, and meditation are just some techniques you can use to take time out and stop. Research by Davidson (2003) showed that even those new to meditation experienced significantly greater activity in the left prefrontal cortex of the brain, an area associated with positive emotion. Importantly, these activities can encourage us to get outside of our minds and our thinking and get back in touch with our intuition and our wisdom. We can become more disciplined at focusing on what we feel (rather than what we think), and in this way become clearer on our core values, purpose, and leader identity.

One of the defining characteristics we can observe in effective leaders is the level of mental energy they possess to get the job done. Leadership and positively influencing others require a clear and uncluttered mind, and the ability to consciously pay attention to worthwhile pursuits, behaviours, and areas where you can make a constructive difference. Effective decision making and transformational results are dependent on you being able to be resilient to everyday distractions and remain focused.

This reflection reminds me of a client who put this notion of stopping to the test by engaging in drawing classes. This became her time to de-stress, decompress, and allow her to explore aspects of her creativity in her unstructured time. The lasting impact she experienced was the effect of this simple exercise on her mood and thinking. By engaging in an unfamiliar drawing task, she could feel her mind relax and empty itself of all the usual thoughts. Her focus on drawing an object in front of her allowed her to suspend her usual thinking patterns and walk away from the sessions feeling mentally relaxed and rejuvenated. This time-out meant she felt refocused on her return to the office. Some leading workplaces recognise the benefit of these types of time-out sessions for their people and research supports this development.

Your ability to maintain effective mental energy is important to your success. Whilst the physical impact of the hours and the workload may be significant, the ability to cut through the 'noise' and manage your energy, day after day, is crucial. This is where the clarity of your boundaries comes in. Without boundaries, you run the risk of derailing yourself through sheer output. With boundaries, you can actively manage the areas you want to influence and those that you consciously decide not to.

Boundaries are not often discussed in workplaces, but they are everywhere. They show up mainly when these unspoken expectations have been crossed. For example, working extreme hours when you have set a personal boundary to manage your time effectively is a classic example which can lead to resentment and dissatisfaction. Managing time is one of the biggest boundaries we can set for ourselves. This may be as straightforward as dedicating certain days of your week to certain activities. As an example, many consulting clients have dedicated client-facing days top-

and-tailed with internal office days. This structure allows the teams to follow up on the client sessions and then to prepare for the next ones. We often find that everyone's week, no matter their occupation, has a certain flow. The key is in being able to identify the unique flow and build your boundaries around it.

Derailer 3: Embedded institutional mindsets

Embedded institutional mindset refers to the wide variety of norms and practices that can be embedded in organisational practices which can get in your way and undermine your leader identity. These can show up in recruitment, promotion, and reward practices.

From a recruitment perspective, one example can be the preference for individuals to have an unbroken, linear career. This requirement can form the basis of the role criteria. It can also be reinforced in interview selection where candidates with career breaks do not make the cut. In today's complex world, with the increase in multiple careers, linear career paths are both outdated and unrealistic; however, they are still the norm in many environments.

From a promotion perspective, organisational mindsets can take the form of eligibility criteria which favour one type of organisational expertise over another. The classic career path from Finance and Sales to CEO is a well-worn track. Far less common are the people-focused paths; for example from HR to CEO or cross-functionally from Finance to Sales. There are many assumptions that underpin why these moves should or should not happen; however, these assumptions are too generalised and rigid for the holistic leader mindsets that are required today. Leaders need to be far more than their function.

Reward practices were cited in the Deloitte Human Trends survey of 2015 as another challenge. This referred to the ongoing practice of only offering leader development to the top talent in organisations – a trend that has been embedded forever. At the same time, this practice underpins why organisations feel underprepared in their leadership pipelines. Offering leadership development to individuals at every level is a new mindset that is slowly being adopted into mainstream practice. It is fundamental to building leader capability and managing the complexity of work.

Another aspect of reward and promotion is the mindset that organisational systems are based on merit only. There is now a plethora of research which shows that, at senior levels, there are influences more than merit that are affecting the numbers. The imbalance of the men to women ratio at senior levels – which I have referred to earlier – is what is commonly termed the 90/10 or 80/20 challenge. This ratio highlights that particularly senior promotions are skewed towards the male side of organisational talent. When companies actually do their leadership audit, this realisation comes to the fore and represents another embedded mindset that needs to be challenged. Certainly, a merit-based culture underpins high-performing businesses; however, these companies can only really make merit-based claims when their organisational levels are balanced. Until then, there is a lot of work to do in understanding which other mindsets and organisational practices are impacting their choice of leaders.

Lack of access to flexible work can represent another embedded institutional mindset. Some organisations have understood the power of challenging the full-time view and have taken to offering all their roles with a flexibility option. This, in part, has been driven by the realisation that the next generations will live past 100 years old and work for more than 60. Accessing flexible work and embedding it into the corporate DNA is a way of future-proofing the company. These companies have also recognised that flexible work benefits their entire talent pool. This includes younger workers who value balance, and more experienced employees who may be looking to build more variety into their week. This action has been taken to ensure that men and women take up this option equally. However, these companies are not in the majority, and if you happen to be an individual who needs flexibility but are not in a position to access it, this can represent an ongoing challenge which can derail you from staying true to your leader identity.

Exercise 18: Identifying external derailers

Being able to see potential derailers in your environment is often a 'blind spot' that many people don't realise, until they bump up against them. Derailers can show up in situations such as difficulty in getting promoted, not having access to informal networks in your workplace, or not having role models or mentors to support your progression. There are too many potential derailers to mention here; however, the following questions should help you to identify whether there are some you need to address:

1. Are career development opportunities equally available to you and others?

2. Is there a variety of role models and people of different backgrounds in your leadership ranks?

3. Are you able to get the cooperation of your colleagues or others when you don't have authority? Does anything get in your way?

4. Can difficult issues be raised in your team without people reacting negatively?

5. Are there gaps in your team in terms of how people are recognised and rewarded?

6. Which assumptions underpin your culture? Or the way people are promoted? Or the access people have to resources? Are these the right assumptions?

The actions you take in managing derailers in your environment do not have to be huge. Here's an example of what one team decided to commit to:

- Listen to everyone – seek different perspectives from people at all levels.

- Grant people permission to lead.

- Walk the floor to get outside views and cross-functional input.

- Start meetings with recognition of individuals who show leadership.

Derailer 4: Self-derailers

This section is dedicated to the potential impact that self-limiting beliefs can have on the way you see yourself and your leader identity. Managing self-limiting beliefs is a challenge common to us all. They are a part of life. We all vary in the beliefs we hold but their existence is universal. A common belief we hear is, "I don't see myself as a leader because I am not in a position of authority." Research shows that you can lead from any position – it is really a matter of choosing to have a positive influence on others.

Typically, it is your self-limiting beliefs which can underpin the negative self-talk that we engage in every day. As you know, when left unchecked, these inner dialogues can destabilise your leadership potential by causing self-doubt and self-censorship. These beliefs and thinking patterns hold us back from going for a promotion, speaking up in meetings, or even staying true to our own values.

Self-limiting beliefs can imbalance our thinking, and in doing so, obscure our view of reality. Their impact can be so great that we can get caught up in how these beliefs make us feel and be derailed from what is important. One client who got caught in this cycle of negativity comes to mind. His company identified him as being ready for a new challenge and he had indicated that he was keen to explore his international options within the group. By the time he was referred for coaching, he had been through six sets of interviews for different roles and his confidence was at an all-time low. It is important to point out that anyone being rejected six times for six different roles would be negatively impacted by this outcome. However, what made this client unique was that he had internalised these knock-backs as akin to someone dying. In his first session, he spoke of wanting time to mourn the passing of each opportunity and to let himself grieve. His whole demeanour was flattened to the degree that he no longer saw the point in pursuing a new path for himself. Delving into his negative self-talk and beliefs, it came to light that he believed he would always be rejected and that each rejection was a reflection of what he 'knew' to be his lack of worth. There isn't time in this chapter to walk through each step in his journey back to confidence and valuing his unique leader identity, however, through reframing, retesting his assumptions, validating his successes, and taking a broader perspective on his desire to move into a bigger, more competitive talent pool, his equilibrium eventually returned. He gradually came to recognise that the beliefs shaped so many years ago were futile and inaccurate. He worked intensively on minimising them and updating them and was eventually successful in managing them as they arose. The fact that he then moved to an international role within the business was an added bonus. This client would be the first to tell you that his inner critic still returns, but in strengthening his leader identity he learnt more effective methods for noticing and minimising its impact.

As you can see in this example, what differs between individuals is how much they pay attention to their self-limiting beliefs. Overcoming these beliefs means learning strategies to reframe your challenges and look for new interpretations or new ways of acceptance. When you say them out loud or write them down, you bring a fresh set of eyes and very often a new way forward. These beliefs are as varied as the people who hold them, so it would be virtually impossible to capture them all here. However, there are some beliefs that seem to arise across context and culture. In our work on leader identity, these have included the following:

- Believing that we have to rely on the leadership of those at the top of the hierarchy to solve our problems or provide our career paths.

- Judging others who do not fit our view of what leaders should look like.

- Believing that our value is not equal to others – the "I'm not good enough to be here" belief.

- Assuming that the biological role of women should determine their workplace opportunities and career trajectory.

- Being afraid to challenge the norms of organisations or teams for fear of retribution.

- Assuming that being socially inclusive without prejudice or judgement is the responsibility of people other than ourselves.

- Believing that men enjoy the relentless 24/7 culture of work and don't require support in creating work practices which fit their life stage equally to women.

- Believing in the media stereotypes of gendered roles and promoting division rather than inclusion.

- Refusing to adapt to changing circumstances because of a belief that this would represent not being authentic.

- Assuming that life is a competition for scarce resources rather than an opportunity to share abundance.

This sample list of beliefs has the potential to undermine your confidence and inflate your self-doubt, making it even more difficult to realise your leader identity. However, the psychology literature is rife with evidence that we are capable and able to challenge our personal beliefs. Our minds are not naturally locked into these belief systems but rather we create them and reinforce them over time. It is our habitual thinking that keeps these beliefs firmly entrenched. However, with sustained effort and awareness these belief systems can be updated. Even the level of happiness in your life is something you can consciously cultivate if you are willing to put in the energy.

It should come as no surprise to you that realising and acting on your leader identity can be enhanced through your own mental training, by building beliefs and wins that support this part of who you are or who you aspire to be. Cultivating beliefs that are more constructive and more conscious can mediate the long-term conditioning that we have all been subject to.

Even in times of adversity there are new and better ways of viewing whichever challenge you may be facing. This is not referring to a simplistic reframe around what you may be learning through the adversity – although this can be helpful. Instead, I am referring to your ability to get some perspective on yourself – to take a helicopter view and notice how you are responding to the challenge. In being able to broaden your perspective, research shows you are more equipped to acknowledge the painful emotions or negative beliefs without becoming locked into them. Noticing and accepting difficult emotions is a core tenet of ACT (Acceptance and Commitment Therapy), which is hugely popular due to its effectiveness.

Susan David takes this concept of self-insight and acceptance further in her work regarding emotional agility. In helping people to overcome the negative emotions that we all experience on a daily basis, she recommends that individuals recognise, label, and accept these and then act from a position of values. Susan's simple four-step process has been helpful to so many individuals caught in trying to manage the potentially undermining effects of negative emotions and unhelpful beliefs.

A healthy, balanced mind is one that is capable of managing these self-limiting derailers and also capable of building strength. It is one that recognises hardship and also celebrates the confidence that comes with clarity on who you are. This does not mean that you will always be free from psychological distress. In fact, sometimes it may mean you need to face adversity in order to grow. However, building your awareness and your clarity of the ways in which you can have a positive influence, provides you with an inner foundation to meet any challenge.

Exercise 19: Identifying self-derailers

To assist you in naming some of the self-limiting beliefs which may be getting in your way, consider the following questions:

1. If you had to summarise the self-limiting beliefs that challenge your confidence, what would they be?

2. If you really were your own best friend, how could these beliefs be reframed as so that they support rather than discourage you?

3. When have you been able to ignore the voice in your head? What did you tell yourself then?

4. Can you look at your self-limiting beliefs objectively and minimise them? For example, are you able to say, "I'm hearing that voice again and I am not going to pay attention to it by ..."

5. How can you reality-test your beliefs? From whom can you seek feedback that will provide you with a different view? How can you welcome positive feedback and make it your own?

6. If you weren't holding yourself back, what would you be doing differently?

Exercise 20: Challenging entrenched beliefs

This exercise is based on the premise that our perceptions of reality – guided by our beliefs – shape our experience. The quadrant below is particularly useful in addressing unhelpful beliefs. This exercise comes from the wonderful work of Dr Anthony Grant at the Coaching Psychology Unit at the University of Sydney. I had the privilege of studying with Tony many years ago in my master's degree and it was his passion and authenticity that spurred my move into my coaching career.

To bring to life how we can start to overcome entrenched beliefs, I have adapted this quadrant by asking you to step through the following questions. With each question I have given you a sample response.

STEP 1: What is an unhelpful belief that gets in your way of having a positive influence on others?

> For example: My opinion is not good enough.
> Your example?

STEP 2: What is the feared consequence of this belief?

> For example: I will be humiliated in front of others.
> Your example?

STEP 3: What do you think is the probability of this event happening?

> For example: Pretty likely, given my team environment.
> Your probability?

STEP 4: How would you rate the awfulness of this event? (10 being truly dreadful)

For example: 8/10

Your rating?   /10

Put your responses to Step 3 and 4 in the quadrant on the next page.

Step 5: Which resources do you have within you that could mediate this outcome?

For example: Personal organisation and preparation.

Your example?

Step 6: Which resources do you have in the people around you to help you avoid this outcome?

For example: I could run my ideas past one or two supporters prior to the meeting.

Your example?

Write your answers to Step 5 and 6 in the quadrant on the next page.

Re-analysis

Describe what could shift in your thinking if you consciously chose to focus on the lower two quadrants and minimised your focus on the top two:

STEP 3: Probability of an event	STEP 4: Awfulness of event
Example: Pretty likely	*Example: 8/10*
Your probability:	Your rating:
STEP 5: Internal resources	**STEP 6: External resources**
Example: • *Personal organisation* • *Planning* Your internal resources:	*Example:* • *Peer support* • *Socialising my ideas* Your external resources:

Clients often find that by *choosing* to focus on the internal and external resources that are available to them, the likelihood or awfulness of an event occurring is minimised. This is because in focusing your attention on your inner resources and the people who support you, you have the capacity to challenge unhelpful beliefs. These are the resources you already have. This awareness will assist you to gradually decrease the impact of outdated belief systems and challenge unhelpful thinking patterns. This self-management approach is a key strategy in managing any self-derailers.

Exercise 21: Addressing your external and self-derailers

Finally, take some time to jot down some of the derailers you may be facing in Figure 8.2. In the middle column you are asked to reflect on the degree to which these derailers may be undermining your leader identity. Are they having an impact on your confidence as a leader or your willingness to step into your potential? To make the best use of this exercise, highlight the top one or two derailers that have the biggest impact. In the third column, write down which actions you could take to alleviate these.

My potential derailers	Impact/10 *Degree to which they are inhibiting my leadership self, where 0=no impact; 10=high impact*	Actions I will take to address these
External derailers: • • • • •		
Self-derailers: • • • • •		

Figure 8.2: Summarising your external and internal derailers

If you want to add additional opportunities for action, use the following summary table to prompt your thinking:

Potential Derailers	Actions I will take
Organisational context	
Life decisions	
Embedded mindsets	
Self-limiting beliefs	

Chapter 9

Realising your unique potential

To be nobody but yourself in a world which is doing its best, night and day, to make you everybody else, means to fight the hardest battle which any human being can fight; and never stop fighting.
– E.E. Cummings

Whatever your path and chosen area of work, whether you are starting your own business or working for someone, whether you are in an office, in the field, in the classroom or at home, whether you are an individual contributor or global entrepreneur, there is one foundational element that will guide your success, and that is *trust* – being trusted and being trustworthy. We all aspire to be treated as we treat others, to be respected, to have people be inclined to act on our ideas, to feel involved, to be challenged, to be listened to openly, and to be valued. These behaviours all come when people trust you. As you gain greater clarity on your unique leader identity and share this consistently, this trust will grow.

In this chapter, I have put together a series of reflective exercises for you to continue your unique leader development and to take proactive ownership of your leader identity. This section is designed for you to build on your leadership approach, assisting you to be successful over the longer term. I would like you to consider each of the exercises in terms of your personal/professional circumstance and brainstorm your own personalised solutions.

As you know, leadership in today's complex world means valuing the collaborative, relationship-focused, and diverse aspects of leading that every individual has the potential to express. As we have mentioned, you can think of this simply as a shift from hierarchical leadership to relational leadership. That is, leadership only comes to life when we are in a relationship with others. Your ability to form mutually beneficial relationships and be connected is the cornerstone of leading. It also means that if leadership is about having a positive influence on others, there are as many interpretations of leadership as there are individuals. Each person's claim to being a leader is valid and real.

However, building and refining your leader identity takes time and effort. It needs your conscious commitment to your own development and it requires your honest, disciplined insight into your current reality and where you would like to go.

I would like you to take some time pulling this information together in a way that is meaningful to you. You do not need to go through every exercise in this chapter laboriously, but rather choose the exercises that reflect what *you think you need to do for yourself right now*. Once again, it is important to remember that your leader identity is an evolving and ongoing process and it is never too late – or too early – to start the process!

Exercise 22: Clarifying your thoughts so far

We have covered a lot about leadership and people's different interpretations of what it means to them. Hopefully these examples have helped you to reach greater clarity on your own thoughts. Given that clarity is often hard to gain, the following five questions are designed to help you reflect on what we have covered so far and gain a deeper insight into your own mindset. Take a moment to jot down your thoughts to each of them:

1. Having read this far, what is taking shape in your own mind regarding your leader identity and what new connections are you making?

2. What has had real meaning for you from what you've read? This could include what surprised you or what has challenged your thinking.

3. What's missing from your leader picture so far? What is it you're not seeing or what do you need more clarity on?

4. What has been your major learning, insight or discovery so far?

5. If there was one thing that hasn't yet been said in order for you to reach a deeper level of understanding or clarity, what would that be?

Exercise 23: Your leader formation

You may recall we focused on where you were in forming your leader identity in Chapter 4. We also talked about the fact that your leader identity is open to constant change and flux. Rather than viewing this change as a weakness, it is a positive reflection of your openness to continue learning and developing. As we know, this adaptation is a key characteristic of high performers and something that will continue throughout your career. This is an important message as we want to help you build clarity on your leader identity on the one hand and also open you up to adapting your leader identity to changing circumstances when required on the other hand.

The list of questions in this exercise on change-readiness is adapted from research by Dr John Franklin, Director of Clinical Psychology at Macquarie University. This is to help you to more clearly identify your willingness to adapt your leader identity.

Are you able to answer 'yes' to each of the questions below?

Do you:

1. Recognise that you have an aspect of your leader identity which you accept must be worked on?

2. Believe (not just hope) that any changes you choose to make in your leader identity are possible?

3. Have the ability to set specific and realistic goals to realise your leader potential?

4. Accept that you have the primary responsibility for these changes to your leader identity?

5. Have an accurate insight into the real nature and cause of any derailers you may be experiencing in forming your leader identity?

6. Have a willingness to examine and address these contributing derailers?

7. Understand and are prepared to experience some discomfort in the process of making changes?

If you are able to confidently answer 'yes' to the above questions, then you are well positioned to lead successfully, recognise where you need to adapt, and in doing so, maintain your sense of leader self that will deliver the best results.

If you found yourself hesitating over some of your responses, now may be the time to reflect on these and write out some thoughts on addressing them. It may be helpful to ask yourself:

- What actions can I take that may help me feel more comfortable with adapting my leader identity?

- What mindset do I need to adopt?

- What resources can I draw on to help me do this?

Exercise 24: Articulating your unique leader identity

Sometimes in the early stages of a workshop a participant will comment that they cannot see the value in articulating their leader identity. Their view is that it seems awkward or that they can't imagine a time they would use language like this. I always enjoy this conversation because for me it highlights the degree to which individuals are not owning this part of their identity or how they are already showing up.

The reality is that, in time, the people around you will work out who you are for themselves. However, these perceptions can often be clouded or just plain inaccurate. In my experience, those people who take responsibility for who they are and are willing to share this with the people they work with, are the ones who enjoy the most satisfaction. They are confident and willing to take ownership of the things that matter to them, and, not surprisingly, they get results.

These leaders get results because they have recognised that their ability to disclose their interpretation of leading helps them connect with the people around them more effectively. They gain trust and respect by letting people know upfront, 'This is who I am and this is what you can expect from me'. The language they use does not have to be polished or rehearsed; it is rather everyday language which showcases their truth, and in doing so, builds mutual understanding.

Take the comments recently made by a leader who was inducting a team member who was returning from extended leave. He took the time to tell this team member that, for him, leadership was about allowing his team to find their own solutions. He explained that he was not a directive leader but rather someone who was passionate about partnering. For him, partnering with other divisions was the role of the division but his particular interpretation meant that he was keen to partner with his team just as much. He clarified that working with him would involve setting a mutually agreed mission, but that he would rely on the team to find their own way towards achieving the mission. So, what did this simple explanation do for his returning team member? It gave her the confidence to know what to expect and the clarity around the parameters of their future working relationship. It also opened up the dialogue for the returning team member to add her own interpretation of her leader identity. As it turned out, having autonomy was the returning team member's number one characteristic, so these two leaders were aligned right from the start – magic!

How much trust and respect could you gain if you were prepared to own your leader identity upfront and to let your significant others know 'this is who I am and this is what you can expect from me'?

Well, now it is your turn. I would like you to pull your reflections together by completing the following sentences:

I am a leader who believes in …

I live my values by …

I play to my strengths when …

To me, leadership is about …

As a leader you can expect me to …

As the author of this guide you may expect that my own leader identity is by now cast in stone and 100% formed. I hope that it doesn't surprise you to learn that the more I form the words around my leader identity, the more I want to continue to evolve it. For now, here is how I would describe this part of who I am; however, it bears noting that this will change and may change considerably as my life experiences continue:

I am a leader who believes in … the potential of every individual, regardless of their position or title, their age or their race. I believe in the ability of everyone to inspire those around them – if they choose to acknowledge and step into their unique qualities.

I live my values by … being open, honest, and ethical, by valuing people, being inclusive and generous of spirit.

I play to my strengths when … I am engaging with others, building relationships that matter, and helping people find their unique voice.

To me, leadership is about … making a positive difference.

As a leader, you can expect me to … empower others, find ways of collaborating across functions and borders, and validating people where possible.

If you are struggling to find the words or the expression for your leader identity, then perhaps it is time to get a little creative. You could start by mind-mapping all the words of what leadership means to you – everything you know, the lessons you have learnt, and what you know you don't aspire to be. Start with the word 'leader' in the middle of a blank page and give yourself permission to write down whatever comes to mind. Remember that there are no rights or wrongs when it comes to your interpretation of leading – as long as it has a positive influence on others. So, remove any constraints and give yourself the room to express.

You may also be a more visual person and perhaps creating your own leader vision board is a more useful activity. Give yourself permission to cut out pictures, words, quotes, or any other visual cue that helps capture who you are as a leader and what leadership means to you.

Or there may be one picture that captures it all for you – perhaps you can use the various characteristics of the picture to describe all the aspects of your leader identity. I am always surprised and delighted at the inventiveness and creativity of each person's interpretation when we use picture cards in our programs. What is a picture of a highway to some is a metaphor for strategy and far horizons for others. What is a gathering of people is an army for some and protestors for others, and so on.

As leadership is a social process, I would also like you to consider:

Who will you share your leader identity with?, and

How will you prepare for the conversation?

Exercise 25: Identifying your times to shine

In our working lives we can often dismiss the times in our day where we have actually lived up to our leader expectations and let ourselves shine through. In this next exercise, I would like you to list the times in the past week where your leader identity has shone. The starting point is to put these on a list and to be as detailed as you can. Then I am interested in you giving a gut feel as to the percentage of time that these bright spots represent.

I have included the reflections from another client to assist you:

Times when I have been true to my leader identity in the past week:

Activity Example:	List your examples here:
5 client meetings	
2 team 1-1 sessions	
Project management	
Problem solving	
% of time in the week: 60%	% of time in your week: %

I hope that in doing this exercise, you have surprised yourself at the amount of time you are actually living your leader identity. This is very often the case and it is an important realisation that you are already frequently being the leader you aspire to be.

Exercise 26: Ideas for your development

Many HR practitioners from around the world are proponents of what they call the 70/20/10 development rule. This means that:

- 70% of your leader development will generally occur whilst doing your job

- 20% will occur in learning from others (including performance feedback and learning from role models), and

- 10% will occur in formal settings like training programs.

I like to think that in reading this book you are contributing to the 70% of learning that happens on the job by building your capability to identify areas where you can contribute and positively influence others on a daily basis.

In the grid below are some questions to consider.

70% Opportunities to lead in your job	20% Opportunities to learn from others	10% Opportunities for formal learning of leadership
Suggested activities: • Where can you take more responsibility? • Are there forums for you to represent your team or company? • How can you share ownership with others – are there areas where you can partner with them? • Which projects appeal to you? • Which secondments could you access or arrange? • What creative ideas do you have that could tap into the leadership potential of those around you?	Suggested activities: • How can you become involved in activities outside of your area of expertise? • How can you seek more feedback? • Which questions can you ask that give you insight into the business and where you can contribute more? • What mentoring can you take part in? • Which forums can you attend or observe? • Which external networks can you access? (Consider professional bodies, where you may have studied, etc.) • Which seminars could increase your leader knowledge?	Suggested activities: • What training is available to you in your company that would assist you? • What formal learning would extend your capability? • Which external training programs could you access? • Which online programs appeal to you?

Exercise 27: Pulling it all together

Here is a summary of all of factors we have covered in building your leader identity with some final thought starters for you to answer and help pull your thoughts together:

1. Leader identity: How strongly do you identify as a leader?

   Your past is not over – it shapes how you show up today. How are you acknowledging your unique experiences?

2. Change-readiness – Your openness to change, new ways of doing things, and your willingness to adapt.

   How regularly do you read books outside your area for expertise? Or attend seminars outside of it? Or seek views from those who are not experts in your field?

3. Authenticity – Being your authentic self and using your values and strengths transparently.

   What is your one guiding value? How have you used your top strength in the last week? Would those around you recognise it?

4. Inclusion – Your awareness/action in embracing difference and your level of inclusion.

   What would someone of the opposite sex think of your leadership style? Do you seek out people around you to offer different perspectives?

5. Social resources – Building your connections with significant others.

   How can you better recognise the informal mentoring or support you get every day?

6. Validating others – Encouraging others to lead and building a spirit of collaboration.

   Do you know how those around you like to be recognised? How would you rate your praise actions?

7. Organisational derailers – Addressing potential obstacles that may be prevalent in your environment.

   Which assumptions underpin your culture? Or the way people are promoted? Or the access people have to resources? Are these the right assumptions?

8. Self-derailers – Addressing self-limiting beliefs.

   How can you hold off on self-judgement and be a little kinder to yourself?

If you are keen to really understand your own leader identity and to build strategies to strengthen it, you can check out our Leadership ID online self-assessment. You can find it on our website at www.roarpeople.com.au. (Please note this is a paid report.)

Importantly, high performers define leadership on their own terms. They take ownership of how they 'show up' as leaders and are active in communicating their approach to significant others.

Exercise 28: Prioritising action

The first step in any change journey is to **develop clarity** on what it is that you would like to change in building your leader identity and realising your unique potential.

We only have a limited capacity to change our behaviours, so being able to identify what is changing, or what you would most like to change, is important. Often this sense of change can include areas or activities that you have begun changing in the recent past, as it all impacts your overall capacity to actually make the change happen.

To do this effectively, you need to be able to take a 'helicopter view' of your working life and use this perspective to identify the areas that you are either changing or would like to change.

Based on all of the ideas and tips you have read, list the areas that are most appealing to you to change and/or adopt in building your leader identity:

1.

2.

3.

4.

5.

6.

7.

8.

9.

10.

Circle the top 3 areas that will have the most impact on you.

Exercise 29: Realising the benefits

What is your level of conviction to do these three circled activities? High? Medium? Low?

I asked this question at a seminar recently and found myself deferring to the wisdom of the people in the room. The same principle applies to you reading this book. You are a competent individual and the best one to know what you need to do next. For some of you, this book may have been a validation of what you already knew about this part of your identity. Perhaps reading the book has provided a touch point to leader perspectives you have held for years. For others, this book may represent a whole new perspective that requires time to digest. For others, there may be parts of the book that are new and others that are familiar. In all scenarios, I defer to your own wisdom as to the activities you would like to take on. I only ask that whatever you decide to do, you do knowing that you are realising your own unique qualities and making a positive difference to the people around you.

If you are uncertain about making a change or taking ownership of building your leader identity, consider the following questions:

1. What might be the NEGATIVES of doing nothing to developing your leader identity?

2. What might be the POSITIVES of doing nothing to develop your leader identity?

3. What would be the BENEFITS of developing your leader identity?

4. What three steps you can take to develop your leader identity:

i)

ii)

iii)

I am yet to find a quote that beats this wonderful and well-known perspective from Marianne Williamson:

> *Our deepest fear is that we are not inadequate. Our deepest fear is that we are powerful beyond measure ... We ask ourselves, who am I to be brilliant, gorgeous, talented, and fabulous. Actually, who are you not to be?*

When you have spent so much of your adult life on leadership, seeing the good, the bad, and the ugly, it starts to transform your expectations of the world around you and the expectations for yourself. Life's adversity comes in so many distinct shapes and sizes to test your resolve and your beliefs, and this guide is just one resource to help you get on with having a positive influence in the area that means the most to you. The concept of persevering in the face of hardship, of bringing passionate authenticity to your work, of holding yourself accountable, and standing up for your beliefs are foundational leadership principles that will help you to get through any challenge and ultimately to get a glimpse of your own unique leadership potential, of who you are as a leader. Your individual beliefs and passion will make the world a better place. Helping others realise their own leadership potential, one person at a time, will continue that momentum. So thank you for being willing to go on the journey.

Here is a reflection that captures the good work you can do when you are prepared to share your leader identity with others. This is taken from a 16-year-old student:

"Today was an inspiring day. There were great stories on how each person achieved becoming a leader in their own way. It inspires me to accomplish my goals, making sure to make the right choices, and to control my life and path. Thank you for opening up my determination to becoming an inspiring and confident leader."

Who are you as a leader?

References

Avolio, B.J. (2010). *Full Range Leadership Development*, Sage Publications Inc., Thousand Oaks.

Avolio, B.J. and Gardner, W.L. (2005). Authentic leadership development: Getting to the root of positive forms of leadership, *The Leadership Quarterly*, 16, p. 315-338.

Davidson, R.J., Kabat-Zinn, J., Schumacher, J., Rosenkranz, M., Muller, D., Santorelli, S.F., and Sheridan, J.F. (2003). Alterations in brain and immune function produced by mindfulness meditation. *Psychosomatic Medicine*, 65 (4), p. 564-570.

DeRue, D.S., Ashford, S.J., and Cotton, N.C. (2009). Assuming the mantle: Unpacking the process by which individuals internalize a leader identity. In L.M. Roberts and J.E. Dutton (Eds.), *Exploring Positive Identities and Organizations: Building a Theoretical and Research Foundation*.

Dobrow, S.R. and Higgins, M.C. (2005). Developmental networks and professional identity: a longitudinal study. *Career Development International*, 10 (6/7), p. 567-583.

Dutton, J.E., Roberts, L.M., and Bednar J. (2010). Pathways for Positive Identity Construction at Work: Four Types of Positive Identity and the Building of Social Resources, *Academy of Management Review*, Vol. 35, No. 2, p. 265-293.

Eagly, A.H. (1987). *Sex Differences in social behaviour: A social-role interpretation*, Erlbaum, Hillsdale.

Eagly, A.H. and Karau, S.J. (2002). Role Congruity Theory of Prejudice Toward Female Leaders, *Psychological Review*, Vol. 109, No. 3, p. 573-598.

Eagly, A.H. (2005). Achieving relational authenticity in leadership: Does gender matter? *The Leadership Quarterly*, 16, p. 459-474.

Eagly, A.H., and Carli, L.L. (2007). *Through the Labyrinth: the Truth about how Women become Leaders*, Harvard Business School Publishing Corporation, Boston.

Edmonson, A.C., (2012). *Teaming: How Organizations Learn, Innovate, and Compete in the Knowledge Economy*, Harvard Business Review Press, Boston.

Ely, R.J. and Rhode, D.L. (2010). Women and Leadership. In *Handbook of leadership theory and practice: An HBS centennial colloquium on advancing leadership* (Vol. 377). Harvard Business Review Press, Boston.

Franklin, J. (2005). Change readiness in coaching: potentiating client change. *Evidence-based Coaching*, p. 193.

Fredrickson, B. (2009). *Positivity: Groundbreaking Research Reveals How to Embrace the Hidden Strength of Positive Emotions, Overcome Negativity, and Thrive*, Crown Publishers, New York.

Gibson, D.E. (2004). "Role Models in Career Development: New Directions for Theory and Research." *Journal of Vocational Behaviour*, 65, p. 134-156.

Goleman, D. (2001). Emotional intelligence: Issues in paradigm building. *The emotionally intelligent workplace*, 13, p. 26.

Heilman, M.E. (1983). Sex bias in work settings: The Lack of fit model. *Research in Organizational Behavior*, 5, p. 269.

Hewlett, S.A. and Luce, C.B. (2005). "Off-ramps and on-ramps keeping talented women on the road to success" *Harvard Business Review*, 83 (3), p. 43-54.

Ibarra, H. (1999). Provisional selves: experimenting with image and identity in professional adaptation. *Administrative Science Quarterly*, 44 (4), p. 764-791.

Ibarra, H. and Petriglieri, J. (2007). *Impossible Selves: Image Strategies and Identity Threat in Professional Women's Career Transitions*, INSEAD Working Paper.

Ibarra, H., Snook, S. and Ramo, L.G. (2008). *Leader Identity Development*, INSEAD Working Paper

Ibarra, H. (2015) *Act Like a Leader Think Like A Leader*. Harvard Business School Publishing, Boston.

International Labour Office. (2004). *Breaking through the Glass Ceiling – Women in Management*. ILO, United Nations, Geneva.

International Labour Office. (2008). *Remove the Obstacles! On the right track to equality*. ILO, United Nations, Geneva.

Kram, K.E. (1985). *Mentoring at work: Developmental relationships in organizational life*. Scott Foresman, Glenview.

Lord, R.G. and Brown, D.J. (2004). *Leadership Processes and Follower Self-Identity*. Lawrence Erlbaum Associates Publishers, New Jersey.

Markus, H. and Nurius, P. (1986). Possible Selves, *American Psychologist*, 41 (9), p. 954-969.

Markus, H., and Wurf, E. (1987). The dynamic self-concept: A social psychological perspective. In Rosenweig M.R.and Porter L.W. (Eds.), *Annual Review of Psychology*, 38, p. 299-337.

Murphy, S.E. and Johnson, S.K. (2011). The benefits of a long-lens approach to leader development: Understanding the seeds of leadership. *The Leadership Quarterly*, 22 (3), p. 459-470.

Piterman, H. (2008). *The leadership challenge: Women in management.* Committee for Economic Development of Australia, Melbourne.

Random House Dictionary, (2014). Random House Inc., New York.

Rhode, D.L. and Kellerman, B. (2007). Women and leadership: The state of play. *Women and leadership: The state of play and strategies for change*, p. 1-62.

Sealy, R.H.V. and Singh, V. (2010). The Importance of Role Models and Demographic Context for Senior Women's Work Identity Development, in *International Journal of Management Reviews*, Blackwell Publishing Limited, Oxford, p. 284-299.

Skinner, S. (2014). Understanding the importance of gender and leader identity formation in executive coaching for senior women. *Coaching: An International Journal of Theory, Research and Practice*, 7 (2), p. 102-114.

Stets, J.E. and Burke, P.J. (2000). Identity theory and social identity theory. *Social Psychology Quarterly*, p. 224-237.

Tzu, S. (1983). *The Art of War*. James Clavell (ed.). Delta Book, New York.

Underhill, B., McAnally, K. and Koriath, J. (2007). *Executive Coaching For Results*. Berrett-Koehler Publishers Inc., San Francisco.

Zander, R.S. and Zander, B. (2002). *The Art of Possibility*. Harvard Business Press, Boston.

Additional reading – website sources

Brené Brown talk can be found at http://www.ted.com/talks/brene_brown_
on_vulnerability

Centre for Talent Innovation summary can be found at http://www.
talentinnovation.org/publication.cfm?publication=1400

Susan David's co-authored article on Emotional Agility in *Harvard Business
Review*, available at https://hbr.org/2013/11/emotional-agility

More of Barbara Fredrickson's work is available at www.positivityratio.com

Information from Gallup can be found at: Crabtree, S. (2013). Worldwide,
13% of employees are engaged at work. Gallup World, http://www.gallup.
com/poll/165269/worldwide-employees-engaged-work.

Institute of Coaching and their research mandate can be found at http://
instituteofcoaching.org/

Leaders Everywhere Challenge can be found at http://www.mixprize.org/m-
prize/leaders-everywhere-challenge?challenge=14226

Mayer-Salovey-Caruso Emotional Intelligence Test (MSCEIT), is by J. D.
Mayer, P. Salovey, and D. R. Caruso, 2002, Toronto, Ontario, Multi-Health
Systems, Inc.

McKinsey 2012 Leadership report can be found at http://www.mckinsey.
com/insights/leading_in_the_21st_century/why_leadership-development_
programs_fail?cid=other-eml-ttn-mip-mck-oth-1412

Deloitte report can be found at ttp://www2.deloitte.com/content/dam/
Deloitte/at/Documents/human-capital/hc-trends-2015.pdf

Erin Reid's *Harvard Business Review* article can be found at https://hbr.
org/2015/04/why-some-men-pretend-to-work-80-hour-weeks

"An approach to Strengths" can be found at http://www.viacharacter.org/

**To get in touch with the author
and learn more about the approach in this book visit:
www.roarpeople.com.au**

Printed in Australia
AUOC01n1251281216
281759AU00003B/3/P

9 780994 386236